BECOMING BABA YAGA

BECOMING BABA YAGA

Trickster, Feminist, and Witch of the Woods

KRIS SPISAK

FOREWORD BY **GENNAROSE NETHERCOTT**

ILLUSTRATIONS BY **DAVEZILLA**

HAMPTON ROADS

This edition first published in 2024 by
Hampton Roads Publishing, an imprint of Red Wheel/Weiser, LLC
With offices at:
65 Parker Street, Suite 7
Newburyport, MA 01950
Sign up for our newsletter and special offers by going to *www.redwheelweiser.com/newsletter*

Cover art and interior illustrations by Davezilla
Typeset by Sky Peck Design in Adobe Jenson Pro

ISBN: 978-1-64297-051-7

Library of Congress Cataloging-in-Publication Data
Names: Spisak, Kris, author.   Title: Becoming Baba Yaga : trickster, feminist, and witch of the
woods /   Kris Spisak ; foreword by GennaRose Nethercott.
Description: Newburyport, MA : Hampton Roads Publishing, 2024. | Includes bibliographical
references. | Summary: "When darkness, fear, and instability inundate our daily lives, folktale
figures like Baba Yaga speak to the dichotomy of our existence--the hope and the horror, the
magic and the mundane. This book provides an in-depth look at the Baba Yaga mythos and
history through Slavic folklore and is a comprehensive resource for anyone hoping to learn more
about this ambiguous character"-- Provided by publisher.
Identifiers: LCCN 2024009912 | ISBN 9781642970517 (trade paperback) | ISBN
9781612834900 (ebook) Subjects: LCSH: Baba Yaga (Legendary character) | Shapeshifting.
| Folklore--Slavic countries. | BISAC: BODY, MIND & SPIRIT / Witchcraft (see also
RELIGION / Wicca) | RELIGION / Wicca (see also BODY, MIND &   SPIRIT /
Witchcraft) Classification: LCC GR75.B22 S57 2024 | DDC 398.20947--dc23/eng/20240415
LC record available at https://lccn.loc.gov/2024009912

Printed in the United States of America
IBI
10 9 8 7 6 5 4 3 2 1

*For everyone who's ever had a story stay with them,
without knowing why*

Contents

Foreword

I'm often asked, "When did you first hear of Baba Yaga?"

Now, they say there are no foolish questions—but Baba Yaga is inclined to disagree.

There is no "first" with Baba Yaga. There is no "last." Like any good story, she can have no beginning and she can have no end. An end of Baba Yaga would mean the end of tale-tellers, and none of us are willing to admit to that possibility. Not yet.

It's true—I can't remember the first time I heard of the old Slavic crone who travels via mortar and pestle and inhabits a hut on chicken legs, deep in the Russian forest. This feels correct. You do not learn of Baba Yaga; she is all the dark things a child is born knowing.

After all, when we enter this world, doesn't our shadow enter with us? The moment you hold an infant to the sun, you see it, spreading below them like a cloak. Yes, this shadow twin is where Baba Yaga resides.

And yet . . . if ever there were an attempt to track the legend (the way a bird-watcher might track a particularly rare winged beast), this book is it. With *Becoming Baba Yaga*, Kris Spisak presents a robust work of scholarship. Baba Yaga is a wily shapeshifter, nearly impossible to pin down—but Spisak miraculously transforms alongside her, ever keeping up.

The text of *Becoming Baba Yaga* follows the character's literal transformations, yes—from serpent-tailed to bear-clawed, ribbon-tongued to iron-jawed, goat-footed to frog-mouthed. But Spisak goes far beyond the literal. She chases Baba Yaga's origins across Greek mythology, ancient Trypillian deities, and Mordvin funeral practices. Charging through time, we glimpse Baba in fairytales like "Cinderella" and "Hansel and Gretel." Even the tooth fairy makes an appearance. And of course, our friend Baba

Yaga is too stubborn to be confined to the folktale alone. Spisak loyally trails her as she jumps out of oral tradition and into 1930s Soviet cartoons, political propaganda of the 1980 Moscow Olympics, Tolstoy novels, *Scooby Doo* episodes, and even—I'm not kidding—the video games of Sonic the Hedgehog and Mario alike.

In reading Spisak's work, I can't help but think of the Scottish ballad Tam Lin—in which a woman clings tight to her beloved as he transforms into a swan, a lion, a bar of red-hot iron—and refuses to let go, despite the violence of each new creature. I can only imagine the scratch marks this research left on Spisak.

She refuses to let go even when Baba Yaga transforms into Death himself.

I see a folktale as a living thing. It adapts as if alive. It learns from its surroundings and evolves to fit into each new storyteller's mouth. A folktale will alter its markings like a chameleon, blending into each culture and time period that adopts it. It has a desperate desire, it seems, to stay alive.

It's not just in changing form—both in her physical body and her story's genre—that someone like Baba Yaga endures over centuries. She also changes *function*. At times, Baba Yaga is a cautionary boogeyman to scare children away from dangerous woods. In other moments, she becomes a tool for othering—used as antisemitic propaganda with her long nose and hunger for babies. Sometimes she is a healer, and sometimes an exemplar of stranger danger. When culture calls for a take-no-prisoners old woman to look up to, she becomes a role model. After all, a folktale is a mirror, reflecting the taboos, mores, and desires of the people who tell it. There is nothing interesting about what a monster says about being a monster. Show me what a monster says about being a *person*.

In Spisak's words, "There is good; there is evil. Then there is Baba Yaga."

Which brings us, I suppose, to today. What is her purpose *now*?

As I was drafting my own Baba Yaga–inspired novel, little did I know, but an untold number of other novels featuring old Boney Legs were also coming into being at exactly the same time. We authors were not in communication with each other, or even aware of the others' existence. I guess there was just something in the air.

If you feel like you're suddenly seeing Baba Yaga everywhere, you're not alone. While she never truly went away, the character is definitely "in" right now in a way that she hasn't been for generations—especially outside the geographical confines of her Slavic origin. As a folklorist, this jolts me awake. I want to know *why*. Why is Baba Yaga, quite suddenly, the it girl of the 21st century?

I think the answer can be found not only in the present—but in artistic movements of the past.

Let's wander back in time to late 1700s Britain. As the 18th Century drew to a close, Europe bubbled with uncertainty. The French Revolution had wet the streets with blood. The English feared something similar might arrive at their own doorstep. Disease felled poets and politicians, children and laborers alike. And amid it all, the Enlightenment had declared that this would be a time of logic and wit, with no room for whimsy. After all, it was a belief in magic that led to witches hung in public squares, was it not? In the eyes of the Enlightenment, magical thinking—whimsy—was synonymous with ignorance. And ignorance was dangerous.

But the thing is, whimsy is also what keeps us *going*. Imagination. Art. Love. These are the things that carry us through times of terror. And so, in the face of the fear and violence of their age, artists took it upon themselves to bring that magic back.

Enter: Romanticism.

The Romanticism movement—spearheaded by the likes of John Keats, Percy Shelley, Lord Byron, and others—leaned into the enchantment of the world around us, both seen and unseen. The *romance of living*, as the movement's name implied. It resurrected old stories and wove new ones, celebrating flowery supernaturalism. It acknowledged that science has its place, yes, but so does mystery. Because good god, without mystery and wonder—what's the damn point?

Today, we face unprecedented times. Oh, what we wouldn't give for just one precented day! But we play the hand we're dealt. We live in a time of plague. Of imminent climate crisis. Of war and political instability and racist, sexist systems. In the week that I write this, alone, a trans child was killed by classmates. A genocide rages that my own nation is funding. A man self-immolated on the steps of an embassy. I carry a COVID test kit in my suitcase wherever I go. This is not a world of known things.

And so, like the Romantics before us—we find ourselves yearning for magic. Call it escapism. Call it metaphors to make sense of the senseless. Call it mercy. Whatever you call it—call it loudly, like a prayer.

As if in answer, we hear the sound of footsteps . . . a chicken-legged hut clomping through the forest.

Baba Yaga has come to us in our time of need. She brings little red mushrooms sprouting from logs. She brings a return to nature as our cities fill with smog. She brings rules and bargains, and—unlike our uncertain world—honors the deals she makes. She brings darkness, yes—but in a form we can handle. A darkness we can learn from, find comfort in. She takes our fear and, like her own body, transforms it into something else. Something strange and captivating and even beautiful.

And it's not just Baba Yaga herself. The twee-sounding Cottagecore—an aesthetic movement marked by strawberry-patterned aprons and speckled toadstools and picnic baskets and, yes, little chicken-legged huts—is a reflection of this same cultural need. While tempting to dismiss at first glance, Cottagecore could just as easily go by a different name: Neo-Romanticism. This is no frivolity. This is a bid for our own sanity and survival.

Throughout this text, Spisak returns again and again to a certain phrase—a call to action with which Baba Yaga often greets her guests: "*Have you come to do deeds or to run from them?*"

Here, at what may feel like the end of all things, Baba Yaga and her kin bring the magic back. And with that magic comes bravery. Bravery to see wonder amid pain. To never stop searching for meaning in the everyday. To stop running. To stand up. To do the deeds that justice demands be done.

—GennaRose Nethercott
Author of *Thistlefoot*

ACKNOWLEDGMENTS

I have such bottomless respect for the storytellers, museum curators, academic researchers, archeologists, historians, translators, interpreters, and endless others that all have given so much to Baba Yaga's legacy and our understanding of her. Oh, what a library you have collected, and oh, how I was honored to delve in. I cannot name all of the countless voices—across time, maps, and languages—but I remain in their debt, for this work could not have begun without them.

Countless active conversations and research queries went into this book as well, and I remain grateful to so many for their assistance, especially those family members and friends within the Ukrainian community who didn't mind being peppered with questions about subtle metaphors in funeral songs, connections between folk art and ancient times, their favorite Baba Yaga tales, and beyond, even when flour from the *varenyky* we were making dusted our hands and the air around us. Thank you also to those who joined in extended discussions of childhood memories amid recent Easter gatherings and to those long gone who shared so much, all the way back to the days when I was a child pressing the button on a tape recorder, with its tiny cassette tape, hidden on my lap under the familiar hand-stitched tablecloth while the grown-ups lingered over dessert and talked of the old days and witches. Thank you to my brother for not announcing my earliest storytelling research practices to everyone at such parties. You were the only one who ever knew what I was doing.

Thank you to Frank Petroski, Lee Hawkins, and Karen A. Chase for their unwavering faith that I could actually undertake this massive project that I had embarked upon, especially on the days when I wasn't sure if it could even be done. Katharine Herndon and Romi Muzyka Poteryko-Spisak, you have both been early readers and editors for me countless times before, but I appreciate your willingness to dive into the depths of this project with me—and its countless holes that sometimes felt inhabited by Baba Yaga and the anxieties only she could provoke. You both helped me find my way out, thankfully without any candle-lit skulls in my hands. S.D. and D.R., you were both motivational forces, consistently challenging my page counts with your own and ensuring I shaped epiphanies and revelations into attention-worthy narratives when my research led me to fascinating places. Thank you to Patricia A. Smith, who moderated a panel I sat on at the 2022 James River Writers Conference—one of my favorite writing conferences—and proposed a writing prompt that, unbeknownst to her, reshaped my vision of how I could approach elements of this book. Wendy DeGroat, Michael White, and the Russian I and Russian Senior Seminar students at the Maggie L. Walker Governor's School for Government and International Studies, thank you for letting me share my fascination with Baba Yaga with you in early 2023 and for sharing so many of your own favorite pieces of her legacy. You bolstered my passion midpursuit in ways you may not have even realized.

Lisa Hagan, I could not ask for a better advocate and supporter of my words and my literary calling, and thank you, too, to the full team at Red Wheel/Weiser. Bringing this project to life has been personally and professionally transformative in ways I couldn't have imagined when I began.

Lastly, I have so much gratitude for the indie bookstore community. Fountain Bookstore in Richmond, Virginia; Shelf Life Books in Richmond, Virginia; Book No Further in Roanoke, Virginia; The Little Bookshop in Midlothian, Virginia; A Novel Idea in Philadelphia, Pennsylvania; Malaprop's Bookstore in Asheville, North Carolina; E. Shaver Booksellers in Savannah, Georgia; FoxTale Book Shoppe in Atlanta, Georgia; Firehouse Books in Fort Collins, Colorado; Boulder Book Store in Boulder, Colorado; Changing Hands Bookstore in Tempe and Phoenix, Arizona; Lark & Owl Booksellers in Georgetown, Texas; and so many others do so much for the reading and writing communities. I've been honored to be a part of their worlds, and I endlessly applaud their work.

Introduction

When my grandmother was a little girl and took a shortcut through the woods, she kept her head down. The pine needle path before her feet held her full attention. Birdsong tittered and warbled in the branches overhead. The shadows of horse chestnut and silver birch leaves fell in patches, then blankets, then shrouds. But nothing tempted her attention away from her path until she returned to the sunshine. Baba Yaga, the witch of the Eastern European forests, was real to my grandmother. As a child, she knew without a doubt in her mind that Baba Yaga preyed upon the young, especially those who didn't listen, those who broke the rules, those who lived by their own internal compass. What was an imperfect girl to do?

My mother was born across the ocean from Baba Yaga's woods but not her influence. The old witch's presence lingered in threats about straying into the darkness, in sharp words about manners and obedience, yet, whether because my mother was the picture of well-mannered perfection or because the woods near her Winnipeg home weren't nearly as deep, Baba Yaga remained familiar, though less a cause for alarm.

As for me, I always considered the familiar Slavic witch a good tale, an echo of my Ukrainian roots not so different from *kolomyka* circle dances and traditions of *pysanky* eggs at Easter. She was simply there, on the periphery. Stories linger like any other tradition.

However, Baba Yaga has remained a presence on my mind. The old woman, with her legs as skinny as bones, lives deep in the woods in a hut that stands on chicken feet. The structure turns and moves as it likes, but especially away from those who seek to find her. Baba Yaga's broom isn't for flying but for sweeping away her tracks. She is rumored to eat her victims for supper if she thinks they deserve it, but she also features in tales of reluctant kindness, of mentorship, and of fairy godmother-like grace. Isn't it time we all knew her for who she is?

Folktale traditions can be difficult to explore, because how does one capture the whispers at bedtime or recollections told back and forth among family and friends, all of which have been built upon centuries and centuries of tellers? There is good; there is evil. Then there is Baba Yaga. Whether we define her as a witch, a trickster, a goddess, a donor, or an old recluse, she eludes all stereotypes and preconceptions.

Baba Yaga refuses to ever do what's expected. Not only can she toss her magic comb aside to sprout a dense forest of trees, but she'll give it to you to help you escape your greatest fear if she deems you worthy. Not only does she use the bones of the dead in the construction of the fence around her home, but her house can stand up and walk away if greater privacy needs dictate.

I cannot glorify a character so ominous and deadly, yet I can't just let her be.

For lean in a little closer. A secret, modern narrative hides between the lines of Baba Yaga's tales.

Her complexities speak to the dichotomies of contemporary existence. Both the world of her origin and our own can be filled with forces of benevolence and malice. Both the natural world and our created societies have attributes to celebrate and to alarm us. Baba Yaga is no life coach, but she has so much to teach us. She's an individual who has harnessed the power of saying no. She takes the idea of being an independent woman to new heights—or new depths, if you consider her stories including holes that plunge into the crevices of the earth. She's also someone who feels wanderlust. She's a tiny house enthusiast, an advocate of herbal remedies, and a woman who is always stronger and more capable than others acknowledge. Modern ideas with a dark, Slavic twist, no?

We live in a moment of history that is transparently vague. Amid all the information at our fingertips, we are surrounded by so many tales that we don't know where to pay attention. The moment we wrap our heads around one situation, another arises that can complicate or confuse or distract us from the pursuits of our everyday living. Violence, scapegoating, extremism, and hatred haunt our real lives in so many ways more than the fear of a witch in the woods.

Spending time with Baba Yaga—as her captive or as the reader of her tales—allows for introspection and understanding, not only of her history but of our own still in the making. The world works in cycles, movements that return again and again. We have been here before, and we will be here in the future. Underneath it all hums the constant chord of hope and determination for a better world that has thrummed in the heart of humanity since the beginning of time. How have we accessed our fears and extreme anxieties? How have we passed on resilience and bravery to our children? How can we capture mindfulness in our daily choices and integrity amid a world that seems ready to eat us for supper? Baba Yaga speaks to all this and more.

Oral traditions come to us in ways not so different from the old game of Telephone, changing ever so slightly with each mouth that shares the words. The folktales included in these pages follow the same legacy. Rooted in the traditions and language choices passed down by various tellers, they are one more version of the tales—because who's to say what the "correct" versions ever were?

An exploration of Baba Yaga's history and her ongoing mystery is something we all need right now, so let's tuck into her fantastical tales, the facts behind them, and the questions they raise within our own lives.

Whatever intention brought you to this book, I'll pose the same question that Baba Yaga favors: have you come to do deeds or run from them?

No matter your answer, let's go deeper—into the woods, where pale birches stand tall and rigid amid the breeze, where the shadows stretch out like the roots of trees, grasping across the topsoil and weeds then plunging deeper into the earth, beyond and beyond and beyond, to the place where they unite with the darkness and its secrets and its sprites, one of which might just be an old woman, a hag, a *babushka*, a witch, who is there to open her arms, welcoming us in, coaxing us deeper, to do her bidding one more time.

1

"THE HORSEMEN of RED, WHITE & BLACK"

t the edge of the forest, the shadows stretch toward you without finding success. Sunlight shimmers in your hair, on your skin, in your eyes—yet the radiance vanishes the moment you step into the inky darkness. Boughs spread their arms. Leaves unfurl overhead, not a springtime bloom but a net slowly unraveling. The air shifts, becoming wet, filling your lungs with peat and moss and poisonous red-capped toadstools.

Adventures begin here. Quests begin here. Lives are changed in this wood beyond the fringes of the places you've ever been.

A horseman dressed all in white hastens by you at breakneck speed, his neck or yours you do not know. But you don't have a good feeling. Out there, somewhere, the warm rays of the sun greet weary travelers, but not you. You lift your feet over gnarled roots, bent like elbows and knees of souls long buried. You duck under pine needles that still brush against you, like familiar fingers trailing your skin. A sticky, sappy remembrance lingers behind each touch.

You've heard of others on this trail, a girl named Vasilisa, a prince named Ivan, but today, only you put one foot forward, then another and another. Your favorite shirt, the one you wear because you've always felt good in it—ready for anything, the protagonist of your story—clings to you now, heavy with lichen that has emerged at its seams.

Another horseman dashes past, this one all in black, as was his horse and its mane and its eyes, though everything has become darker now. How is it possible in the shadows and the mire? You know hours have passed somehow. Night wraps its dusky swathe about your shoulders, even as you try to shrug it off.

You keep lumbering forward, pushing back vines and leaves and tendrils of tree species not yet discovered—because that's what heroes do within their stories, forgetting any duller moments of their lives. The hero persists. The hero keeps on. The hero seeks out the fabled chicken-legged hut and the old woman within, barely contained by its tall wooden beams.

The hero forges their own path over streams and stones, always awaiting the third horseman, dressed all in red—for only with him comes the dawn, the new day—though admittedly never any promise of a happily ever after.

CHAPTER ONE

Clues to Explore

Have you ever had a day where you blink and the sun is up? You take a few breaths. You turn around, and noon's sun blazes down. Then somehow, as if no time has passed at all, twilight surrounds you. Darkness falls. And the day, which had only begun, has slipped past.

Time is a complex element within Baba Yaga's stories, yet even the first time I heard of her horsemen—the horsemen in red, who brings the dawn; the horseman in white, who brings the brightness of daytime; and the horseman in black who brings the night—they felt familiar. Not only are there echoes of other mythologies in their travels, but some days can be like that, can't they? Weeks and years can rush by. Time flies, not only when you're having fun but when life keeps you on your toes.

These are no twelve horsemen of the apocalypse. They are Baba Yaga's horsemen, controllers of time. Yes, the power in this ancient woman's hand is so much greater than other cannibalistic witches you might know.

Oral traditions are harder to capture than a slip of the tongue, and characters like Baba Yaga don't lend any simplicity to the hunt. Just as we forget that those around us do not see the intentions of our minds and hearts but only our words and actions, Baba Yaga too is a creation of others' impressions. We don't necessarily know her motivations, and that missing element adds to her enigma.

In our own lives, every day, our hearts strike out for the good of the world—or at least the good of our personal worlds in whatever way we can pursue it. Baba Yaga started in the same way. Earth goddess. Goddess of fertility. Goddess of the harvest. Force of regeneration. Caretaker of our ancestors' wisdom. Gatekeeper between life and death, guiding souls through their birthing and dying. Yes, these are a part of her legacy too. Yet time, social movements, and politics do their damage.

Don't we all know it? Though not all of us are recast as crones, as ogre witches, as monsters. At least not on our better days.

However, in true Baba Yaga style, she's a *babushka* (grandmother) who owns her complexities and thrives in them. That's a lesson for all of us. We see your assumptions, world, and here's what we have to say about it. Or not. Actions should speak louder than words, but what if those actions are sometimes compassionate and sometimes malicious? Therein lies the rub.

Baba Yaga's identity drifts one direction then another between places and times, but by traveling back into history and crossing her many inhabited lands, we can gather a better understanding of who she may have been, at least to some tellers of her tales.

In contemporary popular culture, her name and character appear more frequently than we realize. The code name of Keanu Reeves's titular character in the John Wick series is "Baba Yaga" within the dark organization where he operates. *Hellboy* comics and Dreamworks' *Puss in Boots* introduce her as a character. Malware has been named after her, and the literary scene has certainly embraced her many possibilities. My own novel, *The Baba Yaga Mask*, is only one of a long legacy, including Orson Scott Card's *Enchantment* and Diana Wynne Jones's *Howl's Moving Castle* with its parallel to a certain someone's chicken-legged hut. While perhaps unfamiliar to American audiences at first glance, Baba Yaga's presence is increasingly relevant to Western lives.

By trailing her backward through time, not only can we discover how she's been introduced to prior generations; we can also pick up the clues of her origins and countless backstories. Specific episodes of our own lives shape and define us, and the same can be said for a folktale character who has existed in popular culture for hundreds of years, with her roots stretching into past millennia. Storytelling over such time spans is almost inconceivable, but our quest is a noble one—no matter how tangled in linguistic vines and hypothesis-laden thistle.

In a 1979 hand-drawn cartoon created by a Soviet-owned film studio, Baba Yaga and her accomplices tried to block the Olympic mascot, Misha the Bear, from playing in the Games. Released ahead of the 1980 Olympics, the old troublesome witch interfered as much as possible in this twenty-six-minute cartoon, even attempting to become the mascot herself, before entering the competition and comically failing repeatedly. Because the Moscow Olympics were boycotted by sixty-six countries, led by the United States, Baba Yaga's role as interfering nuisance is considered a metaphor for the moment, her bumbling, destructive behaviors a parallel to Soviet impressions of the U.S.

Once again, she's more complex than her face value, as grotesque—or as comical in this instance—as that face may be.

Of course, Baba Yaga was a common figure in Soviet-era cartoons from 1930s onward, often serving the morality tale trope to her child audiences. Be good and follow the rules of a well-organized society or else Baba Yaga will eat you! Big bad wolves and boogeymen historically have their roles, no matter your opinion on child-rearing or nationalistic propaganda.

Baba Yaga was known by the Czech version of her name, Ježibaba, in Antonín Dvořák's opera *Rusalka*, which was first performed in Prague in 1901. While the storyline skews close to Hans Christian Andersen's *The Little Mermaid*, Baba Yaga (as Ježibaba) has one of the best-known witch arias in operatic history, luring in the listener as she offers aid true to her dark forest roots.

Her legacy is as gnarled as the tree' branches that surround her dark forest home, and we love her all the more for it

Close to the same time as Dvořák's opera, Anatoly Konstantinovich Lyadov composed a three-and-a-half-minute orchestral poem "Baba-Yaga" in 1904, following the tradition of Modest Mussorgsky's 1874 orchestral arrangement "Pictures at an Exhibition." The work of Victor Hartmann, an artist active amid the 1860s movement to revive Slavic folk songs, folktales, and traditions of medieval Russia, inspired Mussorgsky's piece. Specifically, one of Hartmann's watercolor pieces on display at the Academy of Fine Arts in Saint Petersburg in 1874, depicted a 14th-century style clock inspired by Baba Yaga's chicken-legged hut. In turn, Mussorgsky's ninth movement in "Pictures at an Exhibition" was titled "The Hut on Hen's Legs."

The Telephone game continues. Art begets art begets art, and I imagine Baba Yaga cackling all the while—whether hovering around creative circles, the audiences that consistently whisper and shrink back from her fame, or the shadowy forests and hidden alleyways of old villages where we might expect to find her.

Yet traveling back one hundred or one hundred fifty years is not really so far, when we know how long Baba Yaga has graced imaginations.

If we step back into the era of the birth of folktale studies, we may well come to know the work of Aleksandr Nikolayevich Afanasev. In his lifetime, Afanasev published nearly six hundred Slavic folktales and fairytales, from the first collection of seventy-four stories in 1855 to a significantly larger tome completed in 1863. Much like the Brothers Grimm, his roots were in academia. History, romanticism, mythology, and nature studies initially piqued his interest, with characters like Baba Yaga and Koscheii the Deathless biding their time in the inkless shadows, waiting for the moment their tales would flow from Afanasev's pen.

Keep Koscheii in mind. Not only will we return to him, but he also was one of Baba Yaga's accomplices during her brief animated stint at the 1980 Moscow Olympic Games.

Meanwhile, Afanasev was unique amid his folktale collecting contemporaries. He didn't merely gather oral tales, changing them to his fancy. He collected versions of the tales, meticulously noting his sources, an invaluable record.

Afanasev was hardly the first of the Slavic fairytale collectors. He had multiple contemporaries, tracing back to the work of Vasilii Levshin, who is considered the first to capture Baba Yaga stories in writing. And we cannot ignore the 1788 comedic opera, *Baba Yaga*, by Prince Dmitry Gorchakov and Mathias Stabingher. Designed for Catherine the Great's royal court, the ancient witch's complex portrayal on stage makes me long to see this performance as it once was. Before the final curtain, Baba Yaga remains the sole character in the spotlight. Was she hunched, clenching a giant pestle? Was she dressed in rags or a gown as black as the dark forests of Russia? So many details are lost to history, even as we do know Baba Yaga closed the show with a solo about a better world that could come to be.

Terror. Hideousness. Hope. Possibility.

Yes, this is Baba Yaga, the witch, the motivational sorceress, sharing a lesson and a hint of optimism for audiences to take home. Members of Catherine the Great's royal court, academics digging into dusty record books, modern readers who've always sensed a shadow aching to step into the spotlight and be heard—this is a character crafted through the ages for you all.

But like someone journeying into the woods, weaving between peeling birch trunks and dew-tipped thorns reaching out to pierce us—we must seek her out still, bracing ourselves as best we can as the pursuit begins to test us. We must creep beyond the easily accessible written records of history and published creativity.

We must track her to places where the forest's onyx shadows are no different from the raven-inspired hues of night, where owls call no matter the hour, reminding us not to approach with demands but with the respect such an ancient elder surely deserves.

In her earliest known written record, Mikhail W. Lomonosov's 1755 *Russian Grammar*, Baba Yaga was noted in an academically designed table, where gods, goddesses, and other deities of the world were connected with notes on their geography. The ancient Slavic god Perun, for example, was related with the Roman god Jupiter. Yet in this first-known textual documentation, Baba Yaga stood unaccompanied, with no comparisons the world over. She might have won me over in this detail alone, but let's pause here for a moment.

This Russian grammar book is the beginning of her written legacy, but she's clearly known to the population that may have encountered her here. Her first known written record is hardly an introduction. She's named among the pantheons of gods and goddesses, no insignificant reputation.

Earlier still, woodblock prints known as *lubki,* popular in the 1600s and 1700s, are our earliest known confirmed representations of her. These decorations, originally fashioned from the carve-able layer of wood under the bark of linden trees, hung in the households of those who could not afford more expensive icons. Commonly sold for only a kopek or two, these simple prints were inked with a mixture of soot and burnt sienna boiled in linseed oil. They decorated homes and told stories, even to those who could not read. Lubki captured biblical tales, historical events, and yes, folktale stories well-known and well-treasured.

According to this artistic record, Baba Yaga was already a familiar character in this time period as well, able to stand on her own pictorially and be clearly identifiable. Imagining a cultural icon, a character captured in imaginations across Eastern Europe, but never written down in words is almost difficult for our modern minds to imagine. We live in an age of endless records, of content creation, and of mass media around every corner—corners both shadowy and well-lit in the sunshine. However, we must remember that literacy was not always as widespread as in the contemporary West. Oral traditions have a much

more extensive history. While harder to trace, these legacies hold equal value to messages preserved in parchment and ink, in chisel and stone. Stories are stories. They hold secrets, mysteries, and tremors of humanity within.

After all of the written and pictorial evidence, we can see how Baba Yaga was a familiar presence in the lives and memories of Slavic people across the regions of present-day Russia, Ukraine, Poland, Slovakia, Belarus, and beyond.

Was she connected with the Siberian bird goddess, known as a midwife? Her beak-like nose and her hut's chicken legs may pay their own subtle homage.

Was she linked with another ancient Slavic goddess, tied to the underworld and known to be seated in an iron mortar like a throne, iron pestle in her hands? These objects didn't grant her flight, but, oh, the relationship is far too palpable to ignore.

Do her roots lie in tales of Jezibaba, associated not with the collection of children's bones after eating them but with the collection of baby teeth? Childhood traditions certainly spark their own tales.

Or should we examine the connection with the ancient being that carried the wisdom of time? She was believed to partner with Death as souls transitioned to the opposite side. Sure, "partner with death" sounds a touch macabre, but when wrapping our minds around the persona who guides souls as they enter life and as they leave it, this last role is among the most profound of all, no?

These goddesses, terrors, and traditions are all likely connections, fragments that rebuild and reshatter to create the disjointed and bewildering existence Baba Yaga has held in minds for centuries. Some scholars even trace Baba Yaga's roots to the pre-Indo-European matrilinear pantheon, and logic exists in these foundations.

I don't know about you, but I'm getting excited to roll up my sleeves and embark on this quest for an ogress witch who may also be a goddess.

Dusk begins to fall. Rustling leaves overhead beckon us into the forest's obscurity. Scholars, academics, folklorists, and weavers of their own yarns link Baba Yaga to countless possibilities. The truth remains somewhere in the tangles of thorns and of threads. The headline can fearmonger to sell more subscriptions and to gain more clicks, but to grasp the entirety of the narrative, more time is required. Baba Yaga's three horsemen should be able to help with that.

Examining ourselves, we know that who we are in any given minute of our lives is shaped by our past and present circumstances. All we have done and all the versions of ourselves we have been coalesce to refine us and define us. A folktale is no different. Baba Yaga's stories exist and evolve, building upon their past derivations and seizing upon the new world, the unique societies that she discovers herself within.

No one folklorist, no one spiritualist, no one story captures Baba Yaga's singular essence. Yet each leaves us clues to explore.

And so we shall.

Is her broom made of birch because birch trees are known as "the mother tree," associated with fertility for centuries? Does this association arise from the tale of how birches were the first saplings that grew after the Ice Age, bringing life back after a frozen, desolate existence? Is it true? I don't know, but wow is that a good story.

When examining folktales, we must always appreciate a narrative well-conceived. Only then do we let our curiosity push us on.

One of my favorite approaches to classic tales is in the tradition of the Ukrainian literary master, Lesya Ukrainka, who reimagined well-known tales with new parallels and purposes. In these pages, I mill Baba Yaga tales with a modern eye, as if I had a mortar and pestle of my own, grinding wheat berries down to bran and flour, crushing freshly picked herbs to release their oils and essence.

Recipes, medicines, and cocktails are known to transform with muddling. Stories do too.

And Baba Yaga has always embraced ongoing personal development.

She could be a goddess, a monster, or a little bit of both. Exploring all the remaining specks and nettles are a necessity, even if they may become stuck in our hair or a part of an old ogre witch's brew. Curiosity is as much at the core of humanity as the desire for story itself, and where curiosity and story combine, you find the story historians whose fingers itch to turn back the pages to reveal more about who we have been, who we are, and what shadows and sparks linger to impact our collective future.

How did Baba Yaga become Baba Yaga, and what does the old woman still have to say to us? Let's find out.

2

"THE BIRTH
of BABA YAGA"

To better tilt the planet's spin, the devil determined the essence of evil must walk the earth.

He imagined all the eels and urchins and wolves and rats whisked together to a froth, but it wouldn't do. He imagined thunder and fog and tar and sludge, but horror, he knew, wasn't the same as the squalid unknown on a charcoal black night.

So the devil stole boots from the best cobbler he knew and set out to find his ingredients.

In a foreign market, a shriek of rage snared his attention. A woman berated a man twice her size as she stepped in front of her children. The big man pussyfooted away, and the children smiled. But the devil swept up the woman for his bag.

Across the globe in a schoolhouse surrounded by fields of swaying wheat, a classroom bully stood up to challenge the teacher. A taunt on young lips. A sneer on the smile. Yet the teacher's eyes narrowed and pierced the self-assured gaze of her pupil, sending the younger feet scurrying back to the desk from whence they'd come. The devil liked what he saw and swept the teacher up.

He swept up a woman, the smartest in a room of arguing voices, who didn't speak up to share the answers she knew. He swept up a woman who punched hard when a stranger pressed a hand to her skin and another who screamed when a man told her to smile. A woman clutching wolfsbane, a wife steeping oleander tea, a green-thumbed gardener who nurtured her bougainvillea full of thorns, a widow who ran her fingers through her grey-rooted hair until it stood up on end, and another who unabashedly cursed and swore and raised her glass again with no shame. A woman who followed her gut, ignoring the advice given. A grandmother that cackled with joy as she slammed her door on the modern world, preferring her mortar and pestle, her woodfire stove, and the blissful silence that came when technology and its constant interruptions disappeared.

The devil dumped his bag of twelve women into a massive cauldron, muddling them in water from an iced-over stream. The fire underneath crackled. The water bubbled then boiled. A clamminess filled the air of the little hut where he did his work, a hut that began to lurch and pull like it wanted to flee.

Then the devil took a giant breath and filled his lungs with the women's steam, a taste like beets or onions or garlic or fire. He took in as much as his immortal body could hold. He held it in for scarcely a second, enough to feel its fury and fight. Then he spit it out. And there before him stood Baba Yaga, the essence of malevolence, from the most evil beings on earth. Or so supposed he. And who would dare correct the devil?

CHAPTER TWO

Spit of the Devil

In the moments before the story begins, as "once" hangs in the air but no words have yet followed, the potential of the universe is at the teller's fingertips. The audience waits, thrilled and enlivened, no matter how old or young. They might not always admit it, but it's true. So many stories. What will be this one? The story of now. The story of this moment.

How would you answer that question?

Of this day.

Of this time.

Of your expectation.

Are there heroes? Villains? Someone with a heartfelt desire?

Hopefully that desire doesn't involve twelve women and the devil.

While "The Tale of the Twelve Nasty Women," as this narrative is commonly referred to, speaks of Baba Yaga's own creation, the original doesn't share any details of the women captured within the devil's bag. These additions are my own. Still, the mere existence of this story is worth a moment more of our attention. The idea that twelve women combined could potentially be evil itself is at once intriguing and disturbing. Or is it a matter of these women's vulnerability and malleability when caught by the devil? Oh, we could take these ideas in several bothersome directions. However, almost all stories have secrets hiding within, and this one has three.

"Baba Yaga, the Bony Leg" was the name of the full poem by Nikolay Alexandrovich Nekrasov that first included this devil spit story. While Nekrasov's version could be based on older traditions, no record or hints of this tale are known before his time. Thus, its late addition into the Baba Yaga canon in 1840 doesn't add any historical weight to this conversation. Nekrasov wasn't a folklorist doing deep academic research in the area. He was a storyteller. He had a really good story—one that caught on like skull-lantern fire—but we've already walked through the old witch's history. When considering Baba Yaga's lifetime, 1840 was practically last week. So secret number one: origin stories don't always come first, and later storytellers don't always realize the discrepancy.

So why start here if the story of the twelve women is clearly an origin tale of hazy bygone creation, one late in Baba Yaga's own character timeline? Well, two more revelations hide in this story's subtext which further ground Baba Yaga as a character in time.

Did you notice the existence of the devil in this story?

Of course, you did. He was right there boiling the women and spitting them out, wasn't he? The devil's mere presence speaks to Christianity's entrance into a region filled with folk practices and different belief systems. The devil had never been a part of Baba Yaga's stories in their earliest tellings.

As Slavic gods, goddesses, and rituals were confronted with a different religion that dared to extricate ancient beliefs and replace them, stories clashed as much as people. The divine feminine was recast as the personification of evil because a patriarchal lens shifted the narrative.

Yes, "point of view" is a conversation for storytellers and historians alike.

But Baba Yaga was never originally in cahoots with the devil.

Koscheii the Deathless, sure. Death himself, quite commonly. But the devil is a Christian character.

This tug-of-war and coexistence of two belief systems is called *dvoeverie*, or double faith. It lingers into the present day in many of the Eastern European regions that birthed Baba Yaga, as well as throughout the multigenerational diaspora of these peoples. I bore witness to the dichotomy of this perspective myself. Our family felt bolstered by the folk art symbolism captured in Ukrainian traditional embroidery and the icons of the Virgin Mary throughout my grandparents' house. However, no matter your ancestry, we see this double faith in fragments of our own belief systems, no matter what they are.

How do we value common sense but also experience a sense of hope and possibility when we find a four-leaf clover?

Why are Easter and Jesus Christ's resurrection in parallel to Pagan springtime customs centered around eggs and bunnies?

Why do we believe in determination and a strong work ethic but also wishes upon stars?

The entrance of Christianity into Slavic regions was long before Nikolay Alexandrovich Nekrasov's tale. Slavic populations began to encounter Christian priests and monks in approximately the seventh century, and between these first encounters and the twelfth century, many aspects of the Christian faith were indeed embraced by great numbers of people. But that didn't mean that ancient rituals ceased. The faiths intermingled. Inherited traditions lingered over time, even when gods, goddesses, and the original mythology itself disappeared with the memories of passing generations.

Our written record of this time is sparse, and what remains is largely from the perspective of the conquerors or rewritten in the style of such grandiose legends, we don't know quite what to believe. Thus, vestiges of the past transformed into demonized relics or absorbed into new mythologies.

The wearing of a cross around one's neck to keep you safe from Baba Yaga, who hated such religious amulets, simply became a part of the story.

The act of spitting over one's left shoulder three times to protect against the evil eye when someone compliments a child lingered, while the rationale for doing so was forgotten in time. And for the record, my grandmother never truly spit, for that would be rude. She merely pretended to, because the pretending too would preserve us all.

However, let's return to the secrets of the twelve evil women. Their existence as an origin story is murky. Their plot reminds us that Christianity's entrance into Baba Yaga's world recast everything. And still, these women have one last discussion they beg to begin amid their boiling.

A legacy lingers when it comes to combinations of "evil" or "great" individuals. In the medieval period, the "Nine Worthies" were well known, nine figures from history that represented the chivalric ideal. They were examples to honor and to strive toward.

The first written record we have of them is in Jean de Longuyon's 1312 poem, *Voeux du Paon* ("Vows of the Peacock"), but the concept of these men manifested for centuries in myth, history, and the arts. If you've ever been introduced to medieval European tapestries, you might have come across this tale. Nekrasov, if he was well educated, would have been familiar with it as well.

These "Nine Worthies" were fascinatingly split into divisions: three Christian (King Arthur of Excalibur fame; Charles the Great, emperor of Germany; and the famed crusader Godfrey of Bulloign, known to be called the king of Jerusalem), three Jewish (Joshua, aid to Moses and later leader of the Israelites as they entered the Promised Land; David, who slayed Goliath; and Judas Maccabeus, who led the Maccabean Revolt and preserved Judaism against Hellenistic influences), and three Pagan (Hector, son of Priamus, king of Troy; Alexander the Great; and Julius Cæsar). Definitions of *Pagan* aside—oh, don't you worry; we'll absolutely return to that word—these were the ideal personas for all men to aspire to.

Side note: did you know that the Russian term *czar* (also spelled *tsar*) is derived from Cæsar? Storytelling and words alike have their enchantments.

Nonetheless, returning to the Worthies, women, too, had their equivalents, and fascinatingly, they were not women with classically feminine attributes. Amid the reigns of Queen Mary I and later Queen Elizabeth I of England especially, a resurgence of the nine worthy women's stories justified the right of women to govern with intelligence, bravery, and hero-worthy skill. The tales arose centuries before these women's reigns, yet old stories can be the most influential ones. Doesn't Baba Yaga know it too?

The nine worthy women were split between the classical—note *Pagan* is less used with this group—as well as the Jewish and the Christian. The classical grouping includes Minerva, the Roman goddess of war; Semiramis, a mythical queen of Babylon; and Tomyris, who defeated Cyrus the Great. The Jewish group includes Deborah, a judge of the Israelites; Jael, who killed the commander of an enemy Canaanite army; and Judith, who decapitated Holofernes. The three Christian worthies include Empress Matilda, who initiated a war against her cousin when he usurped the throne; Isabel I of Castile who united Spain; and Joanna II, who reclaimed her throne after being imprisoned by her husband, James of Bourbon.

These lists were fluid. Shakespeare was known to add Hercules and Pompey to the male list, and others added Bernard du Guesclin, a renowned fourteenth-century French soldier, to bring the number to twelve. The women were even more in flux, with Eboudica, queen of a British Celtic tribe; Æthelflæd, who fought off Viking attacks; Margaret of York, who led the Lancastrians in battle; and Amazon queens occasionally joining the list as well.

This brings us back to Baba Yaga and her twelve evil women, not something to aspire to—though these twelve can claim their place among aspirational morality tales centuries old. While Eastern and Western Europe had vastly different traditions, expanded trading routes and Christianization have their lingering effects. Hero worship and morality are so tidily connected in such tales. Crafting Baba Yaga's birth story as a polar contrast to such well-known stories adds profundity to this new-to-his-time telling. Yes, we see what you're playing with here, Nekrasov.

Rumors linger that young Nikolay Alexandrovich Nekrasov was once asked to leave school early in his education for writing satires of his teachers. Oh little, Nikolay. Did you really? And was this the beginning of it all?

All grown up and ready to take on the world with his pen, Nekrasov wrote collections of folktales in verse early in his career—hello, Baba Yaga—but the poetry that is widely considered his greatest literary achievement holds reverberations of his early efforts mocking authority. Nekrasov's narrative poem, *Who Can Be Happy and Free in Russia?* published in 1879, had the same fighting, kicking, devil's-spit-filled spirit of Baba Yaga in its own way. Thus, perhaps we shouldn't condemn him for his creation of the vat of twelve evil women at all. My own retelling might seize upon his original sardonic purpose. Who's to say a storyteller's true intention? Baba Yaga's ever-evolving existence certainly has us asking this question time after time.

Nekrasov had his own failures he sought to confront through his writing, and isn't this one more reason why folktales and fairytales have carried through the centuries? They expose us to ourselves in ways we're more willing to comprehend with big bad wolves, evil stepmothers, and ogresses in the woods. Mirrors shoved in our faces don't have the same effect. Neither does selfie mode, with or without filters.

We often feel our modern era is so distant from who humanity has been in the past. Technology and innovation rule our busy lives. We are connected the world over, at an instant if we so choose. We are not within the hunter-gatherer societies where early people once thrived, nor are we the medieval nobles or peasants out of the history books. But if we remove the veil of modernity, we have to admit that we are much the same.

We live. We love. We strive. New ideas reshape the world we know. We look for heroes and "worthies." And characters like Baba Yaga remind us that while enlightenment, chivalric ideals, and "happily ever after" may not be part of our story, we should continue to push on. To do better. To be better. To be spit out once again.

Into the castles. Into the woods.

Or, of course, she might eat us. Or so the tales say.

3

"YVASHKA with THE BEAR'S EAR"

ou have heard of Baba Yaga's words but beware her tongue for a different reason. Extending from her mouth, it can unfurl like a ribbon, but like none you've ever known. With that tongue, she stretches out to collect all living below as she flies by above. Or so goes the tale told to the one who told me.

For once a boy was born with an ear not quite right. He was known as Yvashka with the Bear's Ear, because that's exactly what it appeared to be. But life was hard for one who looks like no others—you know the truth of this story—though Yvashka knew one day he could be great if only he had the opportunity to try.

So that's what he did, leaving his childhood home, looking for great deeds to do, and collecting friends along the way who were as unjustly treated as himself. Together, Yvashka with the Bear's Ear and his new companions, Quercillo, Montano, and Moustacho, found no great deeds, but they did find an abandoned hut at the edge of the forest. The wooden house listed to one side as if its beams had shifted their weight. Red mushrooms sprouted in colonies by its door. Inside, its shelves were full of food. And with no owner in sight, they immediately claimed it all as their own.

When you find a prize, you would do well not to abandon it. Or this, at least, is what the young men decided. They didn't dare leave the old house in case someone else were to stumble upon it, so they took turns going out to hunt, always leaving one behind to prepare the day's meal, complemented by the house's own plentiful offerings. They hunted deer and boar and eagles. They found cherry trees and berries of all kinds. But every evening, the meal was gone, and the friend tasked with preparing the feast that day while protecting the house turned pale and silent. No matter which one, no matter which day, each always kept his back to the wall.

"This is Baba Yaga's house," one of them finally whispered. "We should go. We can find someplace new."

"But this is our house now," Yvashka with the Bear's Ear proclaimed. "You all go tomorrow. I will take my turn to stay back to deal with the old witch."

All night he thought of how to trap her. He had caught secret glimpses of his companion's backs and the flesh there that appeared ripped away. The old witch had stolen bites, remaining hungry after devouring all their food. Yvashka had seen the truth, no matter how much they tried to hide it, sidestepping around the table, backing out of the room at the end of the night. He refused to let the same happen again.

By the first light of morning—a light brought by a horseman in red who rode by faster than a blink of Yvashka's sleepy eyes—he knew what he must try.

He wished his friends well in their hunting and took up a jar of honey. Then Yvashka with the Bear's Ear poured the honey down the uppermost limbs of a dead tree that stood in the yard. The top of its trunk had a split that would serve his purpose.

When his trap was set, he tucked himself back in the house. The wooden structure creaked in the wind. Ashes stirred in the cold stone fireplace. When he blinked again, a horseman in white rode by bringing the brightest part of the day, and Baba Yaga stood in the yard, mouth agape, shrieking at the waste of honey.

She stretched out her massive tongue, extending it like a lizard's, toward the top of the tree, where the trunk began to split and the honey spilled down in viscous globs. As soon as her tongue reached its destination, Yvashka threw a log, pinning her tongue to the treetop.

The old witch raged and spat. Her yellow face turned orange then red and spotted. Her hands stretched out like claws, but Yvashka hid himself inside until she exhausted herself. Then, tongue still outstretched, Baba Yaga only glared—though he couldn't tell if she could see him at all through her fury.

By the time Yvashka's friends returned, she had collapsed on the dusty ground, tongue unfurled like the strangest of ribbons, a prisoner to the underestimated boy who always believed in his potential—even if no one else ever did.

CHAPTER THREE

A Sight Terrible to Behold

Some speak of witches like brutes who go bump in the night, yet some tales are much bigger than a single fright. In fact, some famous witches arguably aren't witches at all. They are merely characters so difficult to define that no better word describes them. So, *witches* they become, and they are branded in the public mind ever after.

No pointy hats exist. No brooms are ridden. Different stories favor different accessories and unique physical traits, and here is where Baba Yaga defines herself in ways apart from so many other folklore witches.

In "Yvashka with the Bear's Ear," or at least in the telling translated from Russian by George Borrow in the late nineteenth century, which is the inspiration for my tale, Baba Yaga's tongue is her most prominent detail. Extending for yards and scraping the dust of the ground as she flies through the air, it seizes upon anything alive and yanks it upward to her gaping jaws. Strange? Absolutely. And unlike any other witch I've ever known.

Some have sharp words. Some have sharp teeth. Baba Yaga has both; however, her disconcerting, incredibly long tongue is both her weapon and her downfall. Let's linger with this detail. Somewhere between Yvashka's friends' torture and the honey-smeared trap that ensnared her, Baba Yaga's tongue became a key player in this story. Beyond her waste not, want not attitude—which I love, because who doesn't want to save the honey?—her tongue is the element that made her the villain.

Arriving amid darkness and thunder with her tongue lolling out, she tries to eat all the food and occasionally takes a taste of nearby people. Then comes the ultimate honey deception. The classic tale of "Yvashka with the Bear's Ear" is much longer. Beginning with Yvashka as a boy so strong he accidentally tears limbs and heads from playmates and ending with the escape of Baba Yaga deep into a hole in the earth, where Yvashka quests after her for days, the story is simultaneously unexpected and enthralling. Another popular tale, "Realms of Copper, Silver, and Gold," continues the story through the three kingdoms Yvashka travels underground as he pursues her.

The fact that the 1913 English edition of Yvashka's story that I first read was edited by Thomas J. Wise, the famed bibliophile, collector, exposer of forgeries, and significant forger and thief himself, adds one more murky twist to the tale. As readers, who do we trust? The hero? The author? The villain? Only time tells the difference.

Returning to Baba Yaga's villainous tongue—which is up there with my favorite segues ever—the question arises: has your tongue ever made you the villain of your story? Or if not the villain of the full story, the bully of the scene? The tormenter of the moment? That memory you're reliving right now, whatever it may be: a lesson dwells within it. You're allowed to move on when you've figured it out—well, figured it out and maybe apologized. But don't take Baba Yaga's lead on that one. The kindnesses that follow her treacheries can go very, very wrong. Ask Vasilisa's stepmother about the fire returned to her cabin. Or ask Vasilisa herself, because her stepmother's no longer around to tell the tale.

Countless Baba Yaga tales endure in Eastern European folklore. We'll explore many within these pages, though she's rarely the main character of the narrative. She steps onto the page then off again, mystifying and almost unexplainable.

But let's work on some explaining.

We now know of her tongue, but Baba Yaga's physicality gives us so much more to explore. Her eyes, her nose, her legs, and her greater proportions are the focus of many adaptations, while other features seem playfully captured with no greater weight than the whims of the teller. Nekrasov's tale that spoke of Baba Yaga's birth from the twelve collected women also gave Baba Yaga nose hairs that stretched to her shoulders, fangs, horns on her forehead, massive ears, and deep black holes where her eyes should have been.

Monstrous for sure. The horns are presumably a tribute to the devil, a Christian influence again, much like tales that give Baba Yaga a mouth that stretches from earth to the gates of hell. Nekrasov also claims the old witch has "huge ears," but whether this should bring to mind Yvashka's bear's ears and the related Slavic traditions of bears and their supernatural powers remains unclear.

The deep black holes of her eyes call upon the blindness she has in many tales. If eyes are the window to the soul, Baba Yaga must not have one. Or more likely, her lack of sight relates her with those souls already departed. An old tradition lingers that the dead still exist among the living, but they are unable to notice those alive. Multiple planes overlay the same villages, towns, and forests. Each inhabitant, dead or alive, remains unaware of those so close by but in another dimension. However, Baba Yaga travels freely in both worlds. She's aware of the living and the dead, despite the fact that she too cannot always "see."

We can all be blind to worlds outside our own, but we must find a way to pay more attention. Focusing on ourselves and our immediate surroundings may come from a deeper human instinct for self-preservation, but self-obsession is frequently the modern result of such impulses. Baba Yaga is deeply aware but not solipsistic. Her information gathering about the world beyond herself is the source of her advantage. And when one sense is lacking, another is heightened. For Baba Yaga, this advantage lies in her nose.

Her common remark upon the "human scent" of those who visit her hut deep in the woods is potentially connected to this legacy of blindness. If she cannot see, she relies upon other means. Jack, of beanstalk fame, may have had his giant, who after a "Fee Fi Fo Fum," smelled the blood or bones of an Englishman. For Baba Yaga, the "Russian scent" often reveals her secret visitors.

Moreover, her nose itself is unlike any other. Storytellers love their creativity, and Baba Yaga's nose has seen countless descriptions—shaped of skin and cartilage or iron or wood. Baba Yaga's nose has been a beak so long that crows and owls of the wood see her as a comrade. It clangs as it taps upon the rafters of her tiny hut when she moves in her sleep and when the chicken legs underneath reposition themselves for a cozier roost.

At times, her long nose mocks those who have been ostracized or abused in different eras. We don't need to step back far into history to understand the characterization of minority populations as "the Other." Baba Yaga's beaked or bulbous nose is clear antisemitism in certain versions of her tales. Might we all pay more attention to this reality, in our own time as much as any other.

In a similar vein, using her characterization to ridicule women as a whole has led to the occasionally grotesque and disturbing references to her breasts and vagina. Chauvinistic storytellers in a patriarchal society have manipulated the tales in directions that disparage and satirize the feminine—especially the aging feminine—and these vestiges clearly linger in Baba Yaga's modern inheritance.

The other. The outcast. The old woman in the woods, living her own life in her own way, against the norms of the majority of society. The world reacts badly to such souls again and again. We see similar patterns in talking heads on modern news shows, on social media rants, and in painfully stereotypical depictions throughout popular culture. This old

Slavic witch may or may not be without sight, depending on the telling, but our own awareness cannot remain in the dark.

However, the curiosities around Baba Yaga's strong nose and possible lack of vision linger deeper into time. Over a thousand years ago, ancient priests presided over sacred groves in certain Slavic regions. To give thanks to the multiple deities of the time, people came and presented gifts. Breads, fruits, meats—the greater the sacrifice shared, the more significant the gratitude and resulting favor of deity. Fascinatingly, amid this ancient ritual, smell was an essential matter of the sacrifice. Freshly prepared, aromatic gifts brought greater results than something overripe, something molding, or something rotten.

Tradition held that the nose decided the greatness of the gift. The legacy of Baba Yaga's particular nose could easily have been born in such places. Numerous academics believe so, and I agree. Rituals and beliefs have ripple effects, long after their practice is gone. Baba Yaga is occasionally blind, because her nose tells her everything about how people regard her. That nose's shadow is longer than we first perceive.

Ancestral memory is connected to her nose too. Smell has the strongest connection to memory of all of our five senses. You've likely encountered a scent that brought you right back to a moment and a place of your childhood. Music can have the same déjà vu effect, but our sense of smell has an unexpected weight in our recollections. For an ancient being linked with the knowledge of generations of ancestors, her long nose allows for a deeper awareness.

Here she is again, profound and dare-we-say deadly. We cannot discount the tales where Baba Yaga follows a scent like the best of tracking hounds, preparing for the capture and kill. The dark forest is full of aromas—the leaves, the breeze, the animal musk—but her awareness of what should be and what should not be is consistent.

One of the most famous illustrators of Russian folktales, Ivan Yakovlevich Biliban, explored Baba Yaga's physical characteristics within his work. In a striking blend of colors designed to be arresting with muted touch, his watercolors have been described as "dreamlike." Playing with her varied descriptions, Biliban captures her as a frightening white-haired old woman with hairy, elongated arms and ragged, patched clothing in his 1900 illustration from "Vasilisa the Beautiful." Yes, long arms paired with a humongous head is another common depiction of her. Yet in a 1911 illustration from "The tale of the three tsar's wonders and of Ivashka, the priest's son" by A. S. Roslavlev, Biliban captures Baba Yaga with a wooden nose both the length and shape of a pelican's beak. If these two characters didn't share the same name, their artistic depictions would never connect them. This is the story of Baba Yaga. Her legend carries her. Her physicality's only consistency is in her horror.

Ivan Biliban knew this. As he embarked upon his work with Slavic folktales, Biliban traveled deep into areas of Russia he had never explored before beginning his creative process. Authenticity was essential to him, but how does one capture the authentic when so many iterations of this old Slavic witch exist? In the end, Biliban didn't stick to a single Baba Yaga lore. He allowed his illustrations to be as capricious as the old witch herself, and his work is all the more fascinating because of this choice.

Whether her nose defines the distinction between the living and the dead, the respectful or the not, or as a straightforward means for identifying her supper, her special relationship with scenting the people of Russia comes about time and again. Biliban's own travels acknowledge this pattern.

Much like the Giant smells Jack and his blood of an Englishman, as noted, a symmetry exists with other European folktales. In both of these otherworldly villains, we must ask if they simply smell a human scent or if their noses' palette can distinguish cultural differences, like a sommelier's precision discerning a complex note within a wine.

Baba Yaga does identify those who are Russian, most popularly. In fact, she is often generalized as a Russian witch, and she is that; however, she is not only this. In moments when she is smelling "Russian flesh" or "Russian blood," we must remember how many regions across Eastern Europe tell her tales. The lack of other countries named amid the English translation record is scant by comparison, but this could have everything to do with the history of translations and where the opportunity for such collections was even possible.

Of course, Baba Yaga's physicality is so much more than her eyes and nose. Her most common epithet is "Baba Yaga, the boney-legged," after all. If you think of the old expression of having one foot in the grave, you aren't far off. In some tales, she's known to have one normal leg and one that is skeletal and decayed. Such is the life for the gatekeeper between the living and the dead—this woman who is regularly blind to the world of the living while aware of all beings past and present.

One boney leg. Sometimes, two. Sometimes, her boney legs are just references to her frailty, her thinness, her weakness. Or shall we speak to the connection of these skinny, boney legs and her chicken-legged hut?

Oh, Baba Yaga, your possibilities are infinite.

And we haven't even gotten to Baba Yaga's size. She has been called an "ogress witch," not purely for her hideousness but because of her sheer magnitude. Every so often, merely her head takes on gargantuan proportions. Other instances, her body fills her entire hut, one foot in one corner, one foot in the other, breasts hanging over the rafters, and nose poking out the door.

No, nothing is simple about this old crone—if we dare to name her as such. Because in the midst of seeking out how Baba Yaga became Baba Yaga as we know her today, not only do we have those who shift and exaggerate the stories as they move from ear to ear—be those ears human or bear. We also have to examine the tellers for they can be antagonists themselves.

She is nothing more than an old woman, or she has eyes like beads, teeth like tusks, and hands like bear claws. Some tales speak of her yellow tinged skin, like the color of the mushrooms in the forest. Not the white of portabellas, but the yellow of plantpot dapperlings or golden chanterelles, growing in a clump at the base of a tree in dew-damp grass that never seems to dry. The descriptions keep coming. Naturally, artists like Biliban wouldn't stick to one illustration.

But wisdom and history hide in Baba Yaga's appearance as much as the grotesque. For after all, wrinkles speak to the experiences that have made us who we are. Smile lines, crow's-feet, black circles under our eyes—they happen. She doesn't cover hers up, no matter if others call her disfigured. Plus, there's a sense that she wouldn't judge you for any so-called "imperfections" either.

The debate between ugly and beauty is a subjective matter, but Baba Yaga's narrators rarely leave room for any doubt. Dare we ask what experiences those tired eyes have witnessed? And dare we ask what stresses have strained her body? And does asking such questions of Baba Yaga reframe our observations about those in the world around us?

Oh, yes, let's flip photo-filter perfection on its head and confront all that's lost with the addition of Photoshop, airbrushing, and AI modifications into our lives. The beauty industry has trained us to panic at every blemish and blotch upon our skin—not to mention the rogue gray hairs that appear. We can always respond with creams, with fillers, and with cucumber slices upon our eyes, but amid superficial concerns, Baba Yaga reminds us of the life that brought us here. Passionate pursuits, adventures, sleepless nights, tears, heartache, glimpses of boundless joy and pain between the cracks of the everyday.

When we look at the abundant descriptions of Baba Yaga, we're reminded that scars are histories of pains survived and that no horror need exist in aging. She whispers secrets of confidence amid any external reaction. The few stories wherein she is bent on her own youth seem more a reflection of the society that told the tales rather than her true foundation.

No matter if she's given iron teeth and arms so long her knuckles graze the ground, Baba Yaga never shrinks back. She sees others' reactions but never hides, diminishes herself, or apologizes. I don't know about you, but she makes me sit up a bit straighter, ready to face the day with focused dedication to my pursuits.

Yvashka may best her with honey. Her tongue might be her downfall. But remember that the story continues, no matter what form her eyes, nose, legs, or any other part of her may take. She escapes and lives on, to be drawn in another form or to be reimagined in another story. Folklore witches have their stereotypes, but Baba Yaga is in a class all her own.

4

"BABA YAGA'S BLACK GEESE"

hen Baba Yaga sent out her black geese, children knew to stay inside, but Sergeii was never a good listener. The boy refused to hide away from an ugly old witch no one had really ever seen anyway. His sister, Olga, tugged at his hand, grabbed at his shoulders, and pulled at the tassels upon his new coat when he tried to dodge her.

"They say that," he said. "But you know it isn't true."

Olga studied her brother's tightly set jaw and too big shoes.

"What makes you so sure?" She didn't release the grip on him she'd finally won, pulling him toward their house with its protection of walls and windows and doors. The black geese were coming closer, honking overhead, gliding shadows on the windless afternoon.

"It's a story to trick us, to make us afraid and act how they want us to."

Sergeii shrugged off his sister, running out in the road, his arms open wide.

The black geese flew closer, their calls smooth and unruffled.

"See?" Sergeii said. "I'm fine."

Olga knew exactly who her brother had been listening to. But bluster wasn't the same as wisdom. Confidence inspires but not always as it should. She opened her mouth to say so, but Sergeii's laugh interrupted her. Then the shudder of the air silenced them both.

Hail tumbled from the cloudless sky. The shadow of a massive mortar emerged from the edge of the wood, but when Olga jerked her head to its source, there was nothing more. The hail had stopped falling. Its littered remains sat like misplaced marbles on the dusty road. And the place where her brother once stood was empty. A single black goose feather fell on the settling breeze.

The time had passed to tell her brother to check the reliability of his sources.

CHAPTER FOUR

An Heir of Goddesses

An old Slavic tradition said the world of the dead wasn't under the earth or in the heavens but a place anyone could reach, only no one alive knew the way. The birds knew its location, and they migrated there every year to visit those who'd come before. Yet birds always returned to the land of the living.

Baba Yaga's black geese are presumably born of such traditions. Having the innate knowledge of the natural world and its otherworldly connections, birds were not the ones who guided souls from one place to the other—for this was Baba Yaga's role—but they had an ease of movement between worlds, between planes, between dimensions. They had a connection with the living as well as the dead. Sashaying through the air, well acquainted with each season's breezes, suspending gravity and human imaginations, birds have been long associated with the miraculous.

In fact, a number of animals and specific forms of forest life are frequently Baba Yaga's partners in her pursuits. Her connection with the natural world, the wild, and the very soil of the earth is at the core of who she is. In this way, her home within the ancient beech forests, amid the mountain pine, at the edge of the peat bogs, and in the shadows of the silver fir becomes more than a setting. Her flora and fauna–filled environment is a force in itself and a metaphor for the roles she takes on. And this metaphor has deep roots, plummeting through rich black soil and swerving around earthworms, while the beasts above and below anticipate her desires.

In the tale of "Baba Yaga's Black Geese," the old witch's darker side is on full display. She's not present on the stage, but her black geese serve her role well. Plus, they do make the perfect building block for a fake news and fact-checking conversation. These modifications are my own, one more link in the chain of her stories, one more teller murmuring ideas into the ink-inspired darkness of the night, joining all the whisperers who have come before.

> *Wandering off alone can be dangerous, child.*
> *Don't go too deep into unknown woods.*
> *Be aware of your surroundings, love.*
> *That which appears harmless may not be so.*
> *Far more exists in the world than that which we think we know.*

The simplicity of messaging in such stories is well understood by parents seeking to protect their children and to prepare them for the world in which we live—whether centuries ago or the years still ahead of us, in a world of a small village or a virtual world we have not yet conceived. Adults, too, would do well to remember.

But does resistance rise in your core at such a warning against wandering in the woods? Or is that just me and my Western sentimental heart, with a naturalism ignited by Henry David Thoreau and the British Romantics? Pieces of me can't abide by a fear of such a place. My spirits lift upon the rare opportunity to walk in a forest so dense no signs of humanity remain, fresh air enabling a fresh state of mind. Green stems tickle my legs as I tread a less trodden trail. Ripples of a stream over smooth river stones allow for a serenity hard to find elsewhere in life.

Perhaps growing up in a place without wolves has spoiled me. The bears I've encountered have let me be—with one exception, but that makes for a good story rather than inspiring terror in the natural world. I have experienced my share of the unexpected and the worrisome. Fear and despair have crept into the woods beside me in unfamiliar terrains and in weather conditions I should have more greatly considered, but maybe I have only been lucky in such moments.

My youth embraced the freedom and purity of the Appalachian woods, their stories unknown to me as a transplant to the area. This ancient witch's forests were layered with tales and traditions, with spirits and sprites she knew all too well—the *leshy*, *rusalka*, and so many more depending on geography and what century we choose to explore. Who are we but creations of the environments that surround us, and thus who is Baba Yaga but a creation of the times and places her stories have been told?

Stories upon stories upon stories. This is how humanity prolongs our days and our memories of who we are and who we always have been. And when we look back, not centuries, but further still, Baba Yaga's ancient roots profoundly connect her to the duality of harvest and autumnal sloughing, fertility and decline, and the complicated balance between humanity and the natural world becomes less obscured. Extending our footpaths into unfamiliar terrains heightens our appreciation and understanding of the greater world. Magnified contexts before our eyes reshape our worldview. Thus, let me share more.

There was once a Slavic goddess of the earth named Mati-Syra-Zemlya. Also going by the names Matka Ziemia and Matushka Zeml'ja, she was among the most ancient of the known Slavic goddesses, and to speak to her, you would dig a hole into the ground and whisper into it. She would listen to your prayers or your confessions, your deeds or your last murmurs of life. To make an oath and touch the earth was an unbreakable promise. Mati-Syra-Zemlya's presence was not usually in human form but as the earth itself, though in rare instances as a human woman, her skin was as dark as the fertile soil of these regions. However, ancient Slavic goddesses, like any other, shifted and changed over time. Baba Yaga's black holes for eyes. The deep dark hole within the earth that she hides herself within to escape Yvashka. Echoes of Mati-Syra-Zemlya linger in her tales when we look for them.

Igor Stravinsky, the twentieth-century composer known for works such as *The Firebird* and *Petrushka*, redefined the modernist movement and rekindled Slavic mythology in his ballet *Le Sacre du Printemps*, or *The Rite of Spring*. In fact, the full title of the ballet is *The Rite of Spring: Pictures from Pagan Russia in Two Parts*. He called upon these same roots—not nature as a cycle of seasons, but nature as a female deity well known in Russia. Was it Mati-Syra-Zemlya? Or another named Mokosh, also spelled Mokoš, a Proto-Slavic mother earth deity known for her massive head and her arms that were unnaturally long? Does this sound familiar?

Mokosh was a goddess of the Kiev pantheon. Statues were raised of her, and, in time, her statues fell. One particular statue constructed of her by command of a prince named Vladimir was celebrated at its official placement atop a hill in the year 980, in what is now the capital city of Ukraine. This same statue was ordered to be destroyed by the same prince when he converted to Christianity eight years later. Prince Vladimir is now known as Saint Vladimir the Great, because of his contributions to Christianity in the region, following the lead of his fascinatingly complex grandmother, Princess Olga of Kiev, also known as Saint Olga, but we'll return to her contradictions in later pages. For now, we shall merely recognize that during Prince Vladimir's reign, Mokosh, who was once revered, began her transition into a goddess witch.

Mokosh and Mati-Syra-Zemlya may be independent figures, but some academics believe that Mokosh derived from Mati-Syra-Zemlya. Both have the same epithet, being known as "moist mother earth," a phrase that lingers in songs and hymns of the present day in certain Eastern European traditions.

It has also been suggested that Baba Yaga is merely Mokosh in her old age, when her fertility is lost but her wisdom and connection to the earth remains. Her honor too has been forgotten. She's now reviled, but she has accepted her new role with the dignity she's always possessed.

With oral traditions, we cannot pinpoint the moment of the first Baba Yaga tale—neither the exact place nor the calendar date. We are forced to look for the clues hiding within the traditions and the secrets that linger in the stories passed between generations.

In respect for these goddesses so connected with nature and the earth itself, spitting on the ground was once considered an insult. The earth was what allowed you to live then accepted your bones back into her womb, so thus to spit onto the dirt was understandably a great offense. The profound beauty of this idea strikes me to the core. Life, death, the earth, and this mysterious character intertwine, and my mind races through every *panikhida* (Ukrainian memorial service the day before a funeral) I've ever known. I haven't yet found any connection between the music designed to be sung to transport a soul to heaven, ashes to ashes, dust to dust, but I'm not giving up on this search for a tiny phrasing with long-forgotten Slavic traditions hiding within.

These earth goddesses transformed over time, their stories woven like the spinning threads both Mati-Syra-Zemlya and Mokosh were celebrated for, because these goddesses of the earth were also linked with traditionally female duties of the home, a complex role carried on by Baba Yaga.

Naturally, these two goddesses likely aren't the only female deities who influenced the creation of Baba Yaga over disparate lands and time. In certain regions of Poland and Slovakia, a tradition endures into the present day of burning or drowning an effigy of the goddess Morana in the springtime. Morana, goddess of lush vegetation but also the harshness and death of winter, is destroyed every year to bring about the birth of spring. The ancient belief system may not linger as it once was, but rituals remain.

On the name day of a different ancient earth goddess in western Ukraine and Belarus, digging a hole or ploughing the earth was forbidden until not so long ago, because these acts would be the greatest disrespect to this goddess on her sacred day.

In a nearby Slavic space, an old Russian saying translates roughly, "to strike the earth is to strike your own mother."

This is hardly the end of these stories. Trypillia, also known as Cucuteni–Trypillia, was a civilization that began roughly 7,000 years ago in present-day Ukraine, Moldova, and Romania. With early cities and advanced pottery techniques older than the Egyptian pyramids and far beyond others in their era, their significance is immense, though the modern world isn't well aware of this history. That being said, archeological findings have revealed what seems to be a worship of a female deity or multiple female goddesses in Trypillia's complex civilization. What echoes of these goddesses became Mati-Syra-Zemlya, Mokosh, Morana, and Baba Yaga herself?

Different scholars have linked many figures to Baba Yaga's origin over time, but each one is rooted in nature and the earth, its potential and its duality. The harshness of winters. The rebirth of spring. Some of these earth goddesses also act as judges in matters of justice and social fairness, including Mati-Syra-Zemlya and the Lithuanian goddess Zemyna. They listened to appeals, settled problems in their own way, and did not tolerate disrespect, dishonesty, or treachery. When the written record is scarce, we must follow the clues and our own intuition. We remind ourselves that humanity is as it always has been, seeking the best path forward in whatever way makes the most sense.

In some story or another, the natural world unquestionably became Baba Yaga's domain. By the time of the wooden decorative carvings called lubki in the 1600s, where she graced homes and captured imaginations, she was already well known. When and how exactly, we don't precisely know, but we do know that Baba Yaga stepped into a legacy respected by generations—generations conflicted with belief in Christianity while simultaneously honoring the old ways. Or maybe they didn't see this as a conflict at all.

My grandparents' generation was deeply rooted in two faiths. They knew of witches but went to Ukrainian Catholic mass. My grandmother had a hatred of geese and their darkness but wore a cross around her neck and sang hymns with a strong voice full of sincere reverence.

I never had the chance to ask her about Mati-Syra-Zemlya, Mokosh, or Morana, but Slavic traditions are no more singular than American ones. Different regions have their different inheritances. She could have known all of them or none.

Yet Baba Yaga, in the shadows of the woods, was familiar to my grandmother. The old witch could find you, but she was nearly impossible to discover herself—maybe if her chicken-legged hut felt you approaching, it would turn around or walk away. Maybe she made herself scarce by diving into secret holes that went deep within the earth. She was known to exist on the border of the darkest woods, across the imperfectly defined line between where mortals wander and where mortals are unable to go—with one good leg on the human side and one boney leg beyond.

The wild can be an oasis, but Baba Yaga's wild isn't so. Vines snake and twist about tree trunks. Leaves and needles block out the sun. But like the old woman herself, complications arise. Nature is two-sided, as lethal and destructive as beautiful and inspirational—so much more than the sinister, sunless wood where breadcrumbs are needed to find one's way out. Oops, that's another tale but one not so different from Olga and Sergeii's that we don't recognize it.

Not Baba Yaga but Baba Roga tales from southern Slavic regions echo the candy-loving witch in "Hansel and Gretel" by the Brothers

Grimm. Again, stories scatter like the wind, their influence and dust settling all over.

Which witch came first? Or did it first begin with these goddesses—one, another, or a separate figure we haven't yet discovered? Such chicken-and-egg questions arise over time—though most chickens don't hold up a house on scrawny yellow legs, talons scratching at the moss-covered forest floor beneath.

Our surroundings shape us, but our ancestors do too. They came before and linger in our bloodlines and in the stories we tell each other and ourselves—including tales about birds flying off to the land of the dead and geese scanning the village for troublesome children. Not all of us have goddesses in our lineage, but no one ever said Baba Yaga is like the rest of us.

5

"BABA YAGA & THE HEDGEHOG'S FLOWER"

o matter how old you are, when your mother asks for help, you find a way. Emptying the pantry of herbs that have spoiled. Plucking the weeds and strangling green shoots encroaching on the garden. You support your family as best you can. You go to the market, finding the best produce, picking it up, bringing it to your nose, squeezing it hard enough to choose the right one.

That's what Marusia was off to do, nothing more than buying the perfect turnips for her mother, but Baba Yaga had other ideas. For as Marusia stepped into the shadow of a tree that hung over her path, the witch reached out her twiggy hands and stole the girl away.

"You are a bad girl," screeched Baba Yaga, as they flew through the air while sitting inside her massive iron mortar. Her voice echoed against the metal bowl. "You wandered so far all alone."

Marusia clutched her empty basket tighter to her side.

"I was going to the market for my mother."

Baba Yaga scowled and ground her iron teeth until they sparked. The pestle in her hands clubbed the air as she paddled them forward. Her dress's fabric whipped in the wind. The old witch lengthened the hem with a wave of her hand, covering more of her boney legs.

"If you are good, I cannot eat you," the old witch finally said as they landed with a jarring thump within the shadows of the wood. Bright green moss cushioned their resting spot the best it could. A hedgehog nosing against a fallen log scurried away into the brush and thorny bracken. "But I can keep you."

She dropped the pestle from her grip and stared at her hands, veined and spotted, hairs springing from her knuckles. Then she pushed the girl toward a strange hut nearby. Bees buzzed from a hive. Mice scurried away from the wild onions sprouting near the door.

So Marusia swept the hut that stirred up dust every time its chicken feet moved; she patched old clothing and chopped up perfect turnips like the ones she was supposed to bring her mother. Every day, Baba Yaga flew off in her mortar, pestle in her hands, shrieking about a flower that would erase her years and allow her to live two hundred more, but Marusia barely listened. She dragged her toe in the dirt as she stepped outside, preparing once again to tend to her chores.

"I know this flower," whispered the hedgehog as the girl picked stones out of Baba Yaga's garden bed—and if a hedgehog were to dare to talk, Marusia assumed she should listen.

She squatted low, giving the prickly creature her full attention. Its beady black eyes met her own. The sunlight that pierced the dense canopy of trees expanded around them. Marusia sat next to the garden as she listened, carelessly plucking weeds that dared to grow in the ancient witch's fertile soil.

When the sky rumbled then cracked overhead, the girl jumped. Baba Yaga thumped again to the ground. Red spotted mushrooms leaned away so they wouldn't be crushed. The mice nibbling on wild onions scattered.

"You are a bad hedgehog to share your voice with this girl." Baba Yaga stomped toward them, although even her stomp was aged and tired. "You shall be my dinner."

The hedgehog curled into a ball, only its little brown nose exposed amid its prickles. The witch reached for it anyway, her frail fingernails as jagged at each tip as the creature's quills.

"Wait!" called out Marusia. "He knows where to find your black sunflower!"

Baba Yaga lifted her long nose as if to sniff the truth of the situation. The hedgehog nodded, if it could be called a nod, when his black snout shifted up and down within his prickly ball of armor.

The witch didn't hesitate, sweeping them both back into her mortar and launching them into the air, following the hedgehog's directions as he trembled at the wind. The three traveled for hours or maybe days, until the hedgehog nodded his prickled head toward the ground, where a hidden meadow held a single sunflower that grew as black as tar and as strong as midnight. The old, wrinkled witch traced the lines on her forehead and the creases around her eyes. The flower's seed-filled face was as large as her own, as bumpy and as rough as her own skin.

When she pulled the black sunflower from the earth, the ancient witch became merely a witch—ancient no more. And as she danced and sang a song no one else could understand, she didn't see the hedgehog behind her turn into a boy named Dmitri, who took Marusia's hand and began telling her a new story, the tale of his curse now lifted, the tale that didn't end until they were together at Marusia's mother's table, with the best turnips as the centerpiece of their meal.

Because when vanity meets obsession, everything else can disappear. And true helpers always find a way, in the darkness of the woods and otherwise.

CHAPTER FIVE

Mistress of the Forest, Its Language & Its Creatures

Trading routes and nomadic migration patterns carry much across lands and seas, but fragments of languages and stories are among the cargo. Baba Yaga's multifaceted presence and countless connections to the natural world are likely drawn from these disparate sources. Her narratives parallel nature itself, seeds carried on the wind, deposited wherever they happen to fall. Yet as protectress of the forest, she must be appeased; the power of nature must be respected, or else human life has no chance at all. Moreover, we quickly realize that the animals we meet in her tales are in no way unequal to the hero. Marusia knows it. The audience does too.

Hedgehogs and snakes have their surprises. Mushrooms and trees are more than backdrops. Baba Yaga is at times known to leave the woods, but her identity is tied to the wild, no matter how far she wanders. She's followed by ominous howls and unexplained movements at the corner of your eye. She's awash with mysterious herbal remedies and nonhuman confidants.

In Baba Yaga's woods, fear lingers in the darkness as much as wonder and impossibility. The inspiration for my version of "Baba Yaga and the Hedgehog" is not the only hedgehog tale in Baba Yaga's repertoire. In another, Baba Yaga and a hedgehog argue over a clump of mushrooms—who found them first and thus who gets to keep them. I love the boldness of a hedgehog that will stand its ground against a fearsome witch on matters as simple as mushrooms. And both hedgehog tales have subtexts hiding in etymology and distant though plausibly related mythologies that amplify Baba Yaga's place in the natural world.

Words often have secret histories hiding within them, and the hedgehog's complicated relationship with Baba Yaga begins within the old witch's name. *Baba* is clear enough. I've known many grandmothers who've gone by this title, although you do also see it translated as "old woman" or "old hag." *Granny*, for example, has a similar complication, a dear name for a grandmother or something mumbled under one's breath about a troublesome old woman. Old Russian used the term *baba* as a midwife or sorceress as well, tapping into a deeper understanding of the miraculous nature of birth. A Hungarian witch by the name of Vasorrú Bába is similarly understood as an iron-nosed midwife. But considering all these variances, we have a decent handle on this first part of the old witch's name.

However, *Yaga* remains heavily hypothesized and never quite explained. Seeking word origins can lead you astray when you begin leaning on guesswork. Connections that seem obvious are not always truly there. For example, in English, the *lock* in *wedlock* is not at all etymologically related to a *lock* that secures something safely, although endless metaphors about romantic "keys to one's heart" or conversely "imprisonment" linger around the concept. Moreover, many don't realize that other ostensibly disconnected English terms are indeed related. For example, *grammar* and *glamour* are linked to a shift in the letter *L* and the letter *R* that lingers similarly where the word *colonel* is pronounced like a *kernel* of corn. In short, words have their own abundant stories. Much of my own work plays in this area, digging into etymological holes, language roots, and subtle distinctions. The old witch's love of holes within the earth and hiding amid serpentine roots aside, the second half of her name remains a matter of scholarly guesswork.

Yaga could be nothing more than a simple fictional name, used once and sticking like the heartiest of pine sap to the character who's spanned centuries. Similarly, it could have been a real woman's name linked to such an old story that her real life has been forgotten. Thus, the ancient woman named "Yaga," whoever she might have been, became "Baba Yaga," or "Grandmother Yaga," just as Vira in my novel, *The Baba Yaga Mask*, became "Baba Vira" over the years. Then again, these are not the leading theories. Other etymological hypotheses remain in the realm of possibilities—which are different from the realms of Copper, Silver, and Gold that Yvashka found when he followed Baba Yaga into the depths of the earth.

Yaga has been suggested as a placeholder name for a goddess so revered that worshippers didn't dare utter her true appellation. Thus, *Yaga* could be a substitute word for a true name lost to time. After all, the original Slavic word for bear has disappeared similarly. This forest animal was long revered in belief systems of these areas, and to honor its significance, the bear's true name was considered too sacred to write down. The common spoken word now preserved in history is the once-used placeholder, literally meaning "honey eater" or "honey knower." The allowable word carried on, for with it came no disrespect or unworthy voicing.

I like the idea of *Baba Yaga* as a placeholder name, not so different from those that exist in many other world cultures with such holy names for gods or goddesses that only high priests or priestesses can utter them—and only on the high holy days. Baba Yaga's connections with goddesses are well understood, after all, but I'm not convinced this is our answer.

Returning to the befuddling nature of language itself, the list of *Yaga* origin possibilities becomes long when looking at similar words in the languages where Baba Yaga's tales originated. Sound academic arguments exist around many: *Yaga* has been linked with the words for "disease," "rage," "force," "torture," "venom," "slowness," "worry," "shudder," "horror," "strength," and "understanding." And this is the short list. She has been also associated with the Greek Jason, the Roman Janus, and so many more far-off mythologies. Are these all stretches? Who can say? Baba Yaga herself isn't sharing the secret.

Because the name *Yaga* appears in various forms across different Eastern European cultures, different words fall into place as near matches. After all, she is also Baba Jaga, Iagibaba, Babka Iaga, Jezibaba, Iagaia, Egibishna, Egaboba, Baba-Liaga, and countless other superficially linked derivations of the Baba Yaga name most familiar to world audiences. A Moravian name, ördögbaba, seems to come from the Hungarian word for "devil" or "fiend," *ördög*. A reconstructed Proto-Slavic form *jęga*, seems related to the Indo-European words for "moan" and "torment," linking the idea of Baba Yaga to a "personified nightmare." Scholars like Andreas Johns dig deep into Baba Yaga's etymological possibilities, but when the list begins to grow this long, the only lasting impression is that the world really doesn't know. The only agreement is that she can be truly evil.

The Telephone game goes on, for the worse and for the better. Aleksandr Afanasev, who gave us some of the first written Baba Yaga tales, connected Baba Yaga's name with the Proto-Slavic and Sanskrit word for "snake."

Here's where we return to the hedgehogs that began our conversation. In the Proto-Slavic language, the words for snake and hedgehog—˝Qžь and *ežь respectively—are so close they are easily muddled. Interestingly, the Latin words have the same near spelling and near pronunciation connection, with *echinus*, the Latin word for "hedgehog," and *echidna*, the Latin word for "viper" or "snake." This is an odd connection at first glance, especially when matched in distant alphabets and languages. These Latin words stemmed from the Greek, and if you know your Greek mythology, you might also know of the snake demon, Echidna, who is half woman, half snake. She has a strange parallel with the rusalki from Russian and Polish folklore, who were also commonly half woman, half serpent. Similar hybrid goddesses existed in the Neolithic period in the lands of present-day Ukraine. As for Baba Yaga, her boney legs aren't her only waist-down descriptor. Some tales across time and place have also, intriguingly, given her the tail of a serpent.

Hello, Echidna from Greek mythology? Is the snake demon one more myth that traveled over mountains, seas, and fertile grasslands to become one more piece of Baba Yaga's ancestry?

The fascinating scientific twist is that hedgehogs are one of few creatures on earth that seem to be impervious to snake's venom. Multiple mythologies have drawn from this truth. The snake versus hedgehog relationship, as near linguistic matches and the greatest of antagonists, is a potential battle for the ages. Greek mythology commonly noted hedgehogs as snake killers, and scientific observation shows the same. So when a hedgehog stands up to Baba Yaga fearlessly, even if the character is merely arguing over mushrooms or choosing to share its voice with a girl when it knows it shouldn't, are we seeing one more version of this ageless tale?

There is good versus evil. There is hedgehog versus snake.

Baba Yaga's alternate spelling of *Jezababa* furthers this strange hedgehog-snake connection. The Polish word *jeż* means "hedgehog," but the Polish word *jędza* means "witch," or "fury." You may find yourself asking, what's the deal with all these witchy snake-women? Well, we can at least skip further discussion of the Australian animal known as an echidna, which is a close, albeit spiny, relative of a platypus. This creature is definitively not a part of the Baba Yaga story.

Alternatively, the popular Sonic the Hedgehog video game series also included evil Echidnas that needed to be killed to progress through levels of play. Yes, the hedgehog versus snake story lives on through video game storytelling—although this play on words and stories has its own twist involving aliens, which isn't tied to any historical roots I know.

Russian folklorist and linguist Vladimir Propp called Baba Yaga "mistress of the forest," and I'd say she'd own such a title with pride.

Beyond the rare tales where Baba Yaga is partially a snake, the *Yaga* translated as "venom" or "snake" theory is furthered by tales where she actually transforms into a viper. When she has daughters in her tales, they frequently appear as young women, but they also exist in snake form. In some Eastern European regions, her well-known tales are told with Baba Yaga the witch swapped out of the villain's role, only to be replaced by a nameless magical serpent. Same exact tale, different evildoer. And finally, let's return to Nekrasov, who gave us Baba Yaga's origin from the twelve nasty women. Even Nikolay Alexandrovich Nekrasov gave her a snake-skin coat.

As someone who fears snakes and is a longtime lover of hedgehogs myself, once again I'm forced to wonder if the stories simmering in my bloodline have influenced my opinions on European forest creatures. My discomfort around geese may similarly draw from Baba Yaga's child-snatching avian tales. Either way, I find myself cheering on that hedgehog that helped Marusia find the magic flower and the one that stood up to a witch over mushrooms.

Curiously, the disputed fungi in this story may have a deeper birthright too. We've noted the mushrooms in Ivan Biliban's illustrations and the ones that appeared on the periphery as Marusia did Baba Yaga's requested chores. Red mushrooms with white spots, called fly agaric, seem to have been purposefully inserted into Baba Yaga's written and illustrated tales for centuries. When you were a child and you tried to draw a mushroom, isn't this the precise variety you would have rendered? They hide throughout classic and contemporary storybooks. But these red mushrooms with white spots have storied mythologies in themselves. They were known as the "Mother of Mushrooms" in Baltic mythology and as the source of the earth's creation with the help of a waterbird in Khanty myths. The dots, like warts, are paralleled in the imperfections on Baba Yaga's face.

These mushroom-related tales also build upon myths from western Siberia—both the legacies of wise, elderly female herbalists who practiced in rituals tied to mushrooms as well as the stories of guardian spirits who were half human, half mushroom themselves, who could act as guides to distant realms. Red spotted mushrooms that clumped near birch trees were of particular significance, because birch trees were at times recognized as portals to other worlds for Baba Yaga. This particular fungus was sometime a recognized partner and helper in her movements. The old witch, or wisewoman, or sorceress could move between the lands of the living and the dead, after all. Food for thought next time you see a clump of mushrooms in the forest. Literary legacies remain.

Bringing these ideas into the modern day, I can't be the only one who associates red mushrooms with white dots as magical in the world of Mario and Luigi. Catch one and you can grow bigger and stronger. Plus, their best friend "Toad," is a similar half mushroom, half human creature. Just like in Sonic the Hedgehog, old traditions pop up in the most surprising of ways.

Baba Yaga's all-encompassing natural domain is built upon her legacy of stories, which were built upon stories, which were built upon stories. The oldest ones weren't captured on paper, but even so, trees too have so much to offer. Birches, oaks, and other varieties remain symbolic in Ukrainian folk art in the present day. Birches can represent purity, the feminine, or protection. Oaks can represent strength or courage. Pine needles can represent stamina or eternal youth. Newly unfurling leaves can represent rebirth. The "tree of life" folk art motif captures the past, the present, and the future; our ancestors, ourselves, and future generations to come. The geometric design that captures the roots, trunk, and branches is occasionally composed in a style that appears as a woman with a wide stance, arms raised and outspread. She is called the great goddess or the original mother.

These ideas are distinctive while wildly familiar. As a mistress of the forest with a legacy of goddesses, who protects and may be in cahoots with the many trees, plants, fungi, and creatures that grow within, Baba Yaga too is connected with this folk art symbolism. She preserves the secrets of the years in her own ways.

I've chosen the tree of life design many times when writing my own pysanky—also known as Ukrainian Easter eggs—never initially connecting the symbol to Baba Yaga, but at its essence, the ideas are much the same. And if you noticed the word *writing* rather than *painting* or *designing*, the usage was intentional. The word *pysanky* derives from a root word meaning "to write." Putting together folk art symbols into a message, a story, or a manifesto is at the core of the seasonal tradition.

Every culture has their own way of sharing their values, their identity, who they have been, and who they want to be. I have never seen Baba Yaga on pysanky, but the power of her natural domain in Eastern European culture is often on proud display.

Acknowledging the beauty and power of the places still wild—and how much we can learn when we respect them and pay attention—can fortify us amid the hectic lives we live. Baba Yaga's stories constantly remind us of this. Acknowledging how much of nature remains unexplained reaffirms that as humans we are not at the top of the world order. We are but one more creature who wanders into the forest. The animals and fungi hold equal roles in the story. The words we use can empower us, yet the specificities of human languages are not always as definitive as first assumed. Snakes are ever present, but they can be beaten. And now and again, a hedgehog rooting in the dirt can be our salvation.

6

"BY COMMAND of BABA YAGA"

hen your brother is required to marry the only girl in the kingdom who fits a magic ring, you may assume all won't go well. When the ring was a gift given by Baba Yaga, you may surely be troubled. But when the only girl he can find who fits the ring is you, his sister, you have permission to be horrified.

The old witch evokes terror in countless ways. Teeth of iron. Claws like a bear. Bones of her victims on proud display.

But the ring fit Prince Daniel's sister, Princess Katerina, and the prince declared he must do as the ring commanded. Triangular wolves' teeth carved into the gold encircled the princess's finger, biting at her skin. Or was it her imagination?

Events unfold as they do. A beggar woman's advice. Wooden dolls that sing and shriek. Magic doors that transport lost souls into the woods where they find themselves more astray.

And thus, Katerina found herself precisely there, escaping her determined brother but deep in the forest, hornbeam branches overhead rustling and creaking as they blocked out any hint of the sky. A girl Katerina's own age was there too, rocking in a chair at the window of the strangest house the princess had ever seen. The girl herself was even stranger. Hair the same shade of brown as Katerina's, eyes the same green, hands and fingers remarkably similar as they maneuvered a needle and thread in and out of a blouse's trim, in and out, in and out.

The lopsided hut she sat within lurched, raising itself up on thin chicken's legs, scratching at the dirt, once, twice, before pivoting its front door away. Katerina shrank back, clenching the smooth river stone she always carried in her pocket, a stone she'd found as a young child but always cherished for its simple, strong beauty. But Baba Yaga's daughter, for that was surely who the girl must be, stood and came to another window. Needlework still in hand, she pushed back a tendril of hair disturbed by the hut's commotion.

Those hands. Their sleek fingers that once again pulled her thread taut, again and again. They were the ones intended for the ring. They had been the origin of Baba Yaga's command. Katerina knew without a doubt. Her stupid, stupid brother.

The forest around them quaked. The ground underfoot swayed. Baba Yaga's daughter didn't look up, but she snapped her thin fingers, knowing her mother's magic ways. Katerina felt herself disappear, but somehow not quite so.

"Daughter!" the old witched screeched as she appeared in the yard, "I smell Russian blood."

The daughter raised her eyebrows and looked around, shrugging from her place at the window as she pulled a new needle in and out, as Princess Katerina herself was now nothing more than a splinter of metal in the daughter's hands, being pulled in and out, in and out.

Baba Yaga stomped. She spat. She looked around then finally entered the hut which had turned toward her when she commanded it to do so.

The witch's daughter walked to the door after her mother had crossed the threshold. She stepped outside, looked over her shoulder, and snapped again. Princess Katerina once more became Princess Katerina. The two girls linked eyes then linked hands and began to run, both knowing their own freedom lay far from this place.

When Baba Yaga shrieked out at their footsteps, her daughter reached for the comb in her hair, tossing it over her shoulder as they continued to dash ahead. A thick birch forest sprang up where it landed, white tree trunks straight and dense and tall. The pursuing witch cursed as she weaved and crashed, but it didn't stop her. Katerina reached into her pocket for her stone, squeezing it one last time before throwing it behind her. Yet when the tiny rock hit the dirt of the forest floor, a mountain grew, pushing the witch back and back and back.

Baba Yaga swore and climbed. She tore trees from their roots and boulders from their resting spots. When again she gained on the girls, her daughter threw the blouse she'd been stitching over her shoulder. Its red and black threads became a river of fire, which Baba Yaga fell into. Thus, the old witch burned, though they understood this wasn't her true end.

The pair never knew they had the power to transform the forest and the terrain, to redefine their path and possibilities, but in seeking their freedom from witches, princes, and commands, they reconstructed the world—as brave, determined girls have always done and as is always possible if we throw the right detritus of our lives behind us.

CHAPTER SIX

Transformations

When faced with a situation without any possible happy ending, Baba Yaga enters the scene, and transformation begins. Princess Katerina does not have to marry her brother. Baba Yaga's daughter, once bound, is freed. The world around them literally alters itself because of their desires plus their actions to pursue those desires. Don't you love that combination in a fairytale? More than a wish upon a star, but a wish followed by boots on the ground—or if not boots, I'm sure these girls had some easy-to-run-in footwear.

Once again, Baba Yaga is a catalyst for change while being her unexpected, horrific self. The original tale by Aleksandr Nikolayevich Afanasev is actually titled, "By Command of Prince Daniel," but isn't Baba Yaga the one dictating the commands? In the original tale, or at least the version Afanasev shares, Prince Daniel is given the fated ring by his mother on her deathbed, because Baba Yaga tricked the queen into agreeing to her terms.

Her terms most likely stemmed from the idea that the ring would fit her daughter, of course. Maybe Baba Yaga ensured no other girl in the kingdom had fingers that fit the ring. Maybe she used her magic to guarantee it would be so, casting a spell for miles around the castle, while the sister inside was forgotten. Thus, the plan backfires for all.

Do we have to be challenged to discover what we're capable of? Katerina might not have agreed, but after the awkward proposal and the howling dolls—a horrifying detail I skimmed over, but which remains incredibly creepy—she may see the truth of her ordeal. She was strong before, but after, she can literally move mountains.

While we might not find ourselves in similar predicaments with magic rings and incestuous ambushes, the world presents us with horrors of different kinds. Less sorcery but with equal levels of being aghast at the situations around us. The brutality can feel on par. When reading the latest news from across the world or hearing a breaking story from somewhere not so far away, we understand the shock and horror Katerina is blindsided by. Life was good. Everything was in order. Then nothing would ever be the same. We can't go back to who we were or how the world once existed. We must only find our best way forward.

Notice there's no "happily ever after" in this tale. In life, there never is. But there is making the best of what we've been given, and there's the advantage of linking hands with another who understands.

Transformations are everywhere in Baba Yaga folklore: physical transformations of characters, land, and objects as well as narrative structures that lead to rites of passage of a different kind. Pay attention to the protagonists, for those who meet her also meet their greater potential because of the actions of an ancient witch.

Baba Yaga herself is never the story's leading role, but her consistent position of change agent has led to a description many folklorists have agreed to. She is equated with the existence of a plow, a metaphor perfectly apt, for what does a plow do? It tears up the earth, readying it through force and might to produce new growth. A plow can be brutal, slicing and tumbling about the dirt, but its devastation is for an ambitious purpose, thinking of the future. Having a presence like a plow is both horrible and hopeful. It connects her with the soil of the earth and human invention, which largely sums up Baba Yaga herself, no?

This familiar truth defines Baba Yaga's tales: the horrible witch treats protagonists badly, scares them, and every so often scars them, but she allows their stories to continue. Their lives are shifted in some way because of her actions, and the hero or heroine begins anew after they leave her. Call her a witch or a hag or a cranky old woman, but with the earth as her specialty, she knows the power of tearing things up.

What transformation occurs depends on multiple factors, and once again, trends arise. Specifically, the age of the protagonist and their gender role lead to different reactions from the old witch and different outcomes for the hero or heroine of the story.

When considering child protagonists, for example, we can return to Sergeii and Olga in the classic version of the tale, "Baba Yaga's Black Geese." Their mother tells them not to go out when Baba Yaga's geese are flying; however, they do not listen. In the traditional story, the trustworthiness of the sources aren't the concern, as I twisted the tale, but the horror is in the reality of the witch herself. Sergeii and Olga are both captured within the witch's house in the darkest part of the forest. The brother is caged and prepared for the oven, and the sister creates their escape. If "Hansel and Gretel" again comes to mind, the connection is quite real. This story type is told the world over. The children go somewhere they've been forbidden to go. Something horrible happens, usually involving an evil villain, and in the end, they barely escape with their lives.

While Baba Roga's tale, in southern Slavic regions such as Bosnia, involves offering the children candy, Baba Yaga's tale does not. Hers is not one of trickery but of targeted capture. Tales of the fantastical can be a way for children to process scary realities. Life can be horrifying, but let's not talk about that right now. Let's talk about a witch and a child who can be brave.

Baby fat falls away. We grow. Our innocence is lost because of the world we live in—the world of human creation that we always have lived in. We like to think that modern life is so different from past eras and that, as people, we have evolved so far beyond what we once were, but have we really?

We have technology in our pockets rather than a talisman for luck, but is there a significant difference?

Baba Yaga's stories involving young heroes and heroines are accessible ways not only for children to confront fear and the shadows they're scared of, but also how to proceed with these trepidations. The moral of the story may be that children should heed the advice of their elders, but no matter if we are adults or children, we respond to lessons in stories more profoundly than lessons in lectures. Oh yes, this is the power of the storytellers. Thus, these "stranger danger" tales remind a listening child to be cautious of the outside world, even when all seems fine and when nothing more ominous than birds fly in the sky.

Yet it's also a reprimand and a threat:

Be good or Baba Yaga's geese will sweep you up.
The old witch eats bad children.
Don't stray into the woods because Baba Yaga might find you.

Transformations of strength and the birth of independence, transformation into being better children—Baba Yaga works her magic in so many ways.

However, when the protagonists of her story are adolescents and young adults, different changes come to life. Folktales with teen protagonists fascinate me, because this is the stage in one's life where one begins to challenge leadership figures and come into one's own. The perfect image of a mother dies, and in her place is an overbearing stepmother. A story trope and a mental shift exist all in one. In life, the character herself may not change, but the perception of the mother figure certainly can as a child. And what is a protagonist to do but rebel and wish for earlier days of kindness and naïve understandings of perfection? What is a protagonist to do but try to endure this overbearing new woman forced upon their life, even if she is the same woman she has always been—although let's call her a "stepmother" now because that makes for an easier story to comprehend.

But novercal relations aside—yes, did you know there was an adjective pertaining to stepmothers?—these teen and young adult protagonists find strength they never knew they had thanks to Baba Yaga. Look at Katerina. Look at Baba Yaga's own daughter. Look at Vasilisa shortly to come. They are up against all odds, but they not only survive; they thrive. Baba Yaga is simply the obstacle to overcome in the final stage of becoming their more mature adult selves.

In literature, we speak of coming-of-age stories, but we can also speak to this transformation as a full individualization, to borrow a word from psychoanalysis. The protagonist's identity is well formed, but by meeting new, dramatic challenges through the plot of the story, they access deeper reserves hidden within themselves. Their self-confidence and self-worth are further solidified. Little known strength. Little known bravery. Little known moral fiber in the midst of horror.

The plow tears them apart so that something new can grow.

Stories like this can feed our souls. We listen raptly as young children dreaming of who we will become, as adolescents feeling surrounded by new conflicts, or as adults looking back on the moments that pushed us to become who we are. These instances that shape us continue throughout our lives, don't they?

However, let's return to the ring at the center of Princess Katerina's story, because Baba Yaga's role as a catalyst for coming-of-age tales frequently centers around marriage, at least for the young adult women in her stories. Remember, she is a witch of her time. A young woman's job, in centuries past and in Baba Yaga's geographical footprint, was to prepare herself for marriage: to learn how to cook, how to clean, how to maintain order and wellness, and how to make do with the resources available.

When Baba Yaga catches a girl or a young woman, what does she do? Well, there's always the threat of cannibalism, but when that doesn't happen, the girl's great punishment is not only to take on the daily tasks of the chicken-legged hut, but to do them to Baba Yaga's satisfaction.

And did you catch that big secret? The threat is persistent, but when does Baba Yaga actually win and gobble up the main character? Point me to a single story out of her classic repertoire. The fact that this storyline is actually hard to discover pushes the "Baba Yaga as change agent" theory significantly more. She is horrible as a strategy. She creates terror as a ploy.

We've seen Marusia struggling to complete the old witch's to-do list, but she finds a way to get it done—or at least she does until she meets the hedgehog with its black sunflower secrets. Vasilisa will experience the same self-discovery of bravery, resilience, and her best possible work ethic. Their trial isn't a life-changing quest or battle. Cunning and resourcefulness serve a role, but ultimately, the young women in Baba Yaga's clutches find their escape with their domestic precision. She is a rite of passage, ensuring they find the abilities they need to be successful in their lives.

With young male protagonists, the story changes, as would be expected. With these heroes, she presents herself as a troublemaker and a danger, and the test is not only to conquer her but to do so while protecting others. Yvashka with the Bear's Ear takes up this challenge, as will many a prince named Ivan. She is a trial to overcome, an initiation rite, before the youth can claim his title as a man.

Are these transformation formulas the same in every tale? Not at all. Still, patterns form when we pay attention.

In a similar vein, when objects begin to transform in her tales, the magical potential of everyday items is called into play. Consider the objects Princess Katerina and Baba Yaga's daughter use to transform the forest as they attempt to escape it. No fairy dust or magic wands here— the girls use what they already have at hand. A comb. A stone. A sewing project. Other Baba Yaga tales add to this list of everyday items that can transform someone's possibilities. A handheld mirror and handkerchief can be equally powerful. We'll see these stories soon, where these items, too, become features of the natural landscape that save the moment, reminding the story's audience that we don't need a gift from a fairy god-mother. Everything we need for creating our renewals and revolutions is already within our reach.

Shall we pause here a moment and breathe in the fresh air and pos-sibilities? No matter what we have, we already possess the necessary tools for our redefinition.

Baba Yaga seizes upon the commonplace objects of her time too. A mortar and pestle were once routine instruments in homes and kitch-ens. The stone bowl was used to transform herbs and spices into pastes and rubs, to mash berries to create a compote or jam, to mix medicines into salves and tinctures, to grind wheat into flour, and so much more. Most women of a certain time and place knew these transformational processes well. Perhaps magic is the best way to put into words the inconceivable, the miraculous that's hidden unexplained in the every-day. Women's work has long been called witchcraft to the uninitiated. Is it expertise, precision, or magic? Which makes for the better story? Or if you're Baba Yaga, why not take that mystery and push it further into nonsensical flight?

The secrets of herbs, mushrooms, roots, grains, and other mixable, mashable, grindable substances were minutiae that old ladies who had lived a long time fully understood. An old herbalist and potion maker may indeed have been considered strange or unconventional. Doubts from outsiders, especially from those more entrenched in daily village life, may have crept in about what these old women were really up to. Stories may have arisen doubting their intentions if not their links to humanity itself.

I find myself wondering, how many old women outlived their hus-bands and their dearest friends, transforming their social role—by choice or by circumstance—to the edges of society, where wisdom learned through practice and time was called upon when needed but not truly respected or admired? Here's where we call upon the old proverb: old men become wizards; old women become witches. How many shunned women go into the making of Baba Yaga's tales over hundreds of years or more? Likely many more than the earlier named goddesses. And they all have a role to play.

These women's transformations are worth acknowledging as much as the development of a hero or heroine through the narrative of one of Baba Yaga's tales. When hair isn't kept tidy and the latest fashions are not considered, a forgotten woman could easily transform into a witch, no?

Of course, in rare instances, Baba Yaga herself is the literal object of transformation in her stories. She's been known to become avian and peck at protagonists like a bird, or she becomes a frog or goat to evade capture or detection.

But transformations aren't merely for stories. We continue to be ourselves yet transform constantly, becoming stronger versions of who we are. Can you describe yourself in a single sentence? I can't, although social media profiles have made me try. Furthermore, would that description be the same today as yesterday? What about tomorrow? When challenges, magical and nonmagical alike, are tossed into our own hero's journey, we must remember the old adage, "that which does not kill us makes us stronger." Baba Yaga is the epitome of this idea, though with her, we could always change the spelling for a phrase equally true: "that witch does not kill us, makes us stronger."

Needless to say, the old witch herself has been through more transformations than we can count. Once a goddess, fallen from reverence to a mysterious protector of the forest, then nothing more than an herbalist hiding away, doing the best she can with what nature provides. She witnesses the dark and the light transform every day with her horsemen bringing about the change. She's present for the transformation of life into death and of the beyond into a new life at birth. She seems bent on changing other people, not giving them a say in the matter until she's satisfied that they can be sent off on their way.

Baba Yaga can rage or find the patience of the stars. She can be an old woman or a monster. In her transformations, she might be both. But fear is in the eye of the beholder—or shall we say in the manipulations of the teller of tales? The storytellers have sown the seeds of chaos into something stronger, and we are left with the remains. We can be horrified by them or inspired.

7

"VASILISA THE BEAUTIFUL"

(Part One)

hen Vasilisa was a young child, so young that cornflowers and oxeye daisies fit perfectly into the curls of her hair, her mother pressed a small wooden doll into her hands.

"I cannot stay with you," her mother whispered, her face pale and thin. "But this doll always will."

Vasilisa didn't answer, but she clung to the doll as she nestled closer to her mother who lay nearly motionless in her bed.

"If you ever need help," her mother continued, coughing into her hand once then again, coughs that quaked her frail body under the quilts. She took a breath before starting once more. "If you ever need help or advice, give the doll food and drink and tell it your troubles. It will always assist with anything you might face."

And the words were true.

When her mother died, Vasilisa gave the doll bread to eat and water to drink, and her desperate grief slowly became something she could bear. She bore it as she spent night after night alone with her father who didn't have such a doll for comfort. She bore it when her father married a new wife with daughters of her own. She bore it when her father died, leaving Vasilisa with a stepmother who despised her and stepsisters who pulled on her beautiful curls and flicked dirt onto her smooth skin when they realized how beautiful she was becoming.

When her stepmother beckoned, Vasilisa fetched her the last candle they owned. The shadows of their cottage trembled on the walls as she moved past their splintering kitchen table, past the crookedly embroidered flowers hanging on the wall, past her eldest stepsister, who pursed her thin lips, narrowed her amber-colored eyes at Vasilisa, and blew out the flame.

"You stupid girl," her stepmother shrieked at Vasilisa, ignoring her own daughter's role in the disappearance of the light. "Because of you, we have no more fire. We cannot see. We cannot cook. We will freeze."

"Stupid girl," her stepsisters echoed, their shadows becoming one with the darkness, or perhaps they had always been so.

Vasilisa didn't respond. She never responded to their insults. But she slid her hand into her apron, where after all of these years, she still carried her mother's wooden doll—a secret against any hardship she faced. Vasilisa squeezed the wooden doll. And she didn't know how, but the little doll squeezed her hand back, as it always did.

"You need to fix this," her stepmother howled into the night. "Go to Baba Yaga. She has fire. Don't return until you can bring back the light and warmth that you've lost us."

Vasilisa only nodded. In the darkness, she grabbed a scrap of food from the table and an old, chipped cup before slipping into the night, seeking a sorceress she'd never seen but she'd always known.

CHAPTER SEVEN

A Mentor Like No Other

Vasilisa is the most famous protagonist who encounters Baba Yaga. If you're only familiar with one Baba Yaga tale, this may be the one. For this reason, I've broken her story into two sections, allowing for an intermission of sorts. Before we go any further, certain parallels in Vasilisa's story must be acknowledged. A young girl has lost her mother, and her father remarries a woman who doesn't care for the young child. The marriage brings the addition of two cruel stepsisters into her life, and the absent father doesn't see the girl's mistreatment in the new household. So much familiarity can't be ignored.

We've heard Cinderella tales in stories the world over. These similar protagonists go by many names: Rhodopis in ancient Greece, Le Fresne from medieval France, Chinye from Kenya, Ye Xian of Chinese origin, Zezolla of Italy, Aschenputtel of Germany, and many more across world folktale traditions. They are all persecuted heroines who overcome their downtrodden circumstances. Marriage to royalty or nobility frequently ends the tales, but not always. As for Vasilisa, we will see.

Fairytales do commonly fall into certain patterns, no matter where they are told across the globe. Whether ancient human migratory patterns, later trade routes, or something deep inside our instinctual dreams and desires, the synchronizations become clear. In Baba Yaga's version, the rags to riches tale has multiple unique twists; however, Baba Yaga's persistent role of pushing Vasilisa to be her best self is a particular distinction. The old witch doesn't see goodness within her. She makes Vasilisa prove it repeatedly, which we will soon see. Thus, hard work, gumption, and a motivational-yet-horrifying witch become the three ingredients needed to be at one's best.

That doesn't sound like a formula just anyone can follow, but there's more to take away here.

Being one's best self is different from a coming-of-age tale. Growing up and evolving after conquering different obstacles are truly life-defining. Here's our shout-out to Katerina, Yvashka, and many others. Yet there are the major transformational events of our lives; then there are the small actions we take every single day. They might feel insubstantial at first glance, but little choices add up. Habits form. Diligence, determination, and a drive for excellence aren't the norm. The people who live with such discipline create their own successes.

"Vasilisa the Beautiful" is named such not only for her physical beauty but for how she lives her day-to-day life. Dignity and respect live in such an epithet, and the mentors who have helped her become who she is in the story are with us almost every step of her journey.

The first teachers many of us have in life are our parental figures, and for Vasilisa, this was undoubtedly true. Different versions of this tale allow for different levels of depth concerning her maternal relationship. In some, the story starts when her mother has already died. In others, we see the mother's goodness, gentleness, and love for her daughter in snippets of their life together before she is gone. The doll is a gift with the magic of a mother's love behind it and, on occasion, is even the physical preservation of the mother's soul.

But no matter the version of the tale, the relationship with her mother empowers her and strengthens her. As she grows up, Vasilisa becomes the young woman she is because of this guidance and support. However, she has to feed the relationship too. As the mother relationship becomes the doll relationship, we see this feeding literally with the bread and the water for the doll. If Vasilisa herself does not make the effort, her mentor and aide won't be there to help her. A child cannot solely take, take, take, after all. They must also find their own way to give, for this is as important to their character growth as any other aspect.

Don't you love the subtle messages hiding within popular stories?

As Vasilisa sets off into the woods, Baba Yaga has a unique opportunity for influence. I won't give away the twists of her story, but I will say what you doubtlessly already know: luck has nothing to do with surviving an encounter with the old witch. Instead, she looks for certain character traits, traits that can indeed get you through almost anything. If you are bad, she may eat you, but if you prove your merit, hope endures.

Baba Yaga's stubborn, ill temper demands only the best of others. If someone doesn't meet her high expectations, she will punish them. They will disappear. So sorry, little arrogant Sergeii who didn't believe in her geese, but it's true. She gives protagonists tests to pass: some obvious like the chores she requests of Marusia and others more subtle.

A powerful question I like to ask is if I would pass her tests. How about you? How does examining the character traits she values weigh up against your own personal intentions and your daily actions? Baba Yaga values respect, bravery, intelligence, and integrity. These ideas are always the deciding factors for her. Her assessments are not matters of prowess or major accomplishments won. Instead, they dive into the being at our core and how we demonstrate it.

Weigh each of these traits in your mind: respect, bravery, intelligence, and integrity. Where do you excel? Where might you be lacking? The protagonists of each of her stories face the same challenge, though their success also means their salvation. The meaning of salvation and success is different for each of us, but these simple tenets of character can indeed empower us all.

The first question Baba Yaga asks when someone appears at her gate is often, "Have you come to do deeds or run from them?" It's not a bad question to ask yourself when you wake up in the morning every day. What is your intention? Are you passively reacting to your circumstances or are you actively shaping your day?

If a protagonist answers her first question well, Baba Yaga's horrible appearance in itself is the next test for a hero or heroine to pass. If characters shriek, scream, and run away, or if they gasp at the sight of her, the old witch will react accordingly. Honestly, I love this about her. If someone screams and runs, she will give chase, cackling and shrieking right back at the newcomer. However, time and time again, we are also introduced to characters like Marusia and Vasilisa. These protagonists do not respond to the sight of her by being disrespectful in any way. We'll see the same soon from Natasha and Prince Ivan. If the first interaction is one of respect and kindness, better results will ensue.

Watch Vasilisa's upcoming first interaction with the old witch. Remembering her manners sets the tone for everything that follows. This isn't a spoiler. You knew Baba Yaga was coming.

How you present yourself not only to the world at large but to a wrinkled, misshapen, outwardly powerless old woman makes all the difference. We don't know what our days will bring us, going into the woods, into the office, into school, or into a public square, but how we treat others—no matter who they are or how they appear—can determine so much.

Furthermore, her appearance mirrors the real terror that exists in the world. She captures that hideousness, forcing you to see her as you should truly see the world. When life is alarming, how do we react? She gives us her face as the challenge, forcing us to decide what our action will be. Before any words are said, what is our instinct?

Another trait she demands of those she encounters is bravery. We see it in Vasilisa as she prepares to do what she must and seek the old witch. We see it in Marusia who doesn't scream or whine but deals with her circumstance with as much grace as she can muster. Yvashka faces her to protect his new friends, and again when he follows her into a hole that emerges into new kingdoms deep within the earth in the extended version of the tale. The hedgehog prince once struck down by magic dares to give her advice, which may also bring him to the black sunflower of his own salvation. The old witch respects bravery in surprising ways, but again, she is consistent.

Conversely, bold arrogance is not the same as bravery. Sorry again, Sergeii, and sorry too to Yvashka's friends. If you meet the old witch with swagger and hostility, she might indeed take a bite out of you.

All the same, respect and bravery are not enough, Baba Yaga also requires intelligence if the protagonists of her tales are to survive. Remember that in the longer version of Yvashka's tale, Baba Yaga escapes from his honey trap. She doesn't come after the young man with the bear's ear, as one might guess. Instead, she lets him be. He earned her respect with his trap's cleverness. Divergent thinking and creative problem-solving empower the hero.

For many other characters, like Vasilisa to come, Baba Yaga likes to lay out impossible challenges. They are created for failure, but when the cleverest find ways to succeed, she always honors her word.

Yet after all of this, her threat does not go away. Just because today you were respectful, brave, and smart, that doesn't save you from terrible events tomorrow. Tomorrow, Baba Yaga may eat you up. She remains a constant threat, but isn't that life?

The last measure may be surprising for an old witch bent on her own ways, but Baba Yaga requires a deeper goodness from those she encounters. Her black geese fly out to look for disobedient children after all. Moreover, she's ready to make Marusia her dinner until she learns the girl was actually running an errand for her mother. If only being good were the defining line between our safety and our demise. Vasilisa doesn't believe it for a second but continues being her best, beautiful self. Her multiple mentors have always encouraged such choices.

Forget the black hat, though there may be a broom—this is a witch with a bigger story than a Halloween haunting. Baba Yaga can be mystifying, but in her demands of the protagonists she encounters, she is constant. In these ways, the old witch is less evil and more of a guide. Imagine the toughest trainer you've ever met at a gym. Then fuse that spirit with the forest's inky darkness, the sharpest of its holly prickles, the most poisonous of its berries, fungi, and ivies.

We could all use lessons for "adulting," lessons for personal or professional success, lessons for raising children, and lessons for fulfillment and satisfaction. We have how-to posts on the internet and "life hacks" galore, but true wisdom is a different matter.

Horrible events happen. Horrible circumstances happen. Heck, horrible people sometimes happen. How we respond to the situation at hand is what makes all the difference. Are we respectful? Are we steadfast and brave? Do we have grit, gumption, and intelligence behind our actions? Do we stay true to our moral compass and kind to others, no matter how they may present themselves to us?

Classic Cinderella tales may stretch across the world, but when Baba Yaga is involved, she measures so much more than wishes upon stars. Forget matters of luck. Instead, consider matters of steadfast endurance when the world feels ready to eat us up. For Baba Yaga, the protagonist has to prove themselves to be worthy of such "happily ever afters," if such an ending were to exist.

Her repulsion at the smell of people might be because people so rarely meet her high standards. Humanity as a whole can be quite disgusting. But not all of us—for some of us venture forth demanding more of ourselves, no matter the actions of others. Call it fierce discipline or fear of a witch's response. No matter, we will continue to strive all the same. Fictional and true characters can grow all the stronger for Baba Yaga's ways. Satisfy her expectations or she may gobble you up, the strangest of life coaches indeed.

Recasting our own struggles as nothing more than an old witch challenging us to do better gives us back the upper hand. And what will we do with it? That's for you to decide.

8

"VASILISA THE BEAUTIFUL"

(Part Two)

hose magic was more powerful? The witch lurking somewhere out there in the wood or her own mother's spirit, who lived in her doll and in her blood, steeling Vasilisa's courage and the muscles in her legs as she kept walking? Her father had told her about the old babushka who had more power in her boney hands than the bringer of death himself.

Vasilisa blew out a breath, seeking ancestral fortification. The power of every determined woman who came before her settled around her like a cloak. The darkness of the wood was only darkness. Her own shadow fell tall and brash across the others.

Around another bend, a stream ran as cold as midwinter, even on this early autumn night. Vasilisa crouched by the bank, careful to keep her boots and the hem of her dress away from the rippling water. She pulled the little wooden doll from her pocket and set it on a clump of moss. After dipping her chipped cup in the stream, she offered a scrap of food and the drink of water to the doll, begging for its protection, before she forced herself to stand again.

The moon escaped its swathe of clouds and shone down upon her anew as she set out on her way. Silent owls' wings stirred the air. Pine needles brushed against her like the fur of beasts.

Vasilisa shifted another bough aside. This time, she didn't meet more shadows. Before her stood a small hut, circled by a fence of tall white bones. Perched at intervals along the fence were human skulls with flickering firelight inside, illuminating the space amid the night's coal black darkness. The hut slowly stood from its roost, stretching out its scrawny legs, stirring loose a few white feathers, before resettling itself on the ground facing a new direction. Facing her.

Vasilisa remembered the house that stood before her from her father's tales. The fence of human bones. The chicken legs. The house of Baba Yaga.

The front door creaked, a long nose appearing from within before anything else.

"Who comes to seek me?"

The witch's voice brought goose bumps to Vasilisa's skin. Vasilisa clutched the doll in her pocket and the doll clutched her back as she answered, explaining her stepmother's request.

Baba Yaga narrowed her eyes, turning toward the many lights surrounding her house, like a scavenger cherishing her spoils.

"I will give you light," the witch continued, scratching her chin with a long fingernail, "if you prove yourself first."

"Of course!" The words burst out of Vasilisa faster than she meant them to. "Of course I will . . . madam." She wasn't sure how to politely address the woman but knew some form of respect was required.

Baba Yaga might have smiled then or it might have been a web of shadows across her jaw. She again tapped her chin with her long fingernail before explaining the tasks Vasilisa would need to complete in a day's time.

Tidy the hut. Scrub the bone fence. Cook a feast enough for twelve men, for Baba Yaga was very hungry.

Vasilisa nodded. She could do it. She knew she could do it. She tried to ignore the ravenous glare in the witch's eyes as Baba Yaga summarized the requested menu for her meal.

"And," Baba Yaga added. The old witch heaved up a massive burlap sack that had been inside her doorway, strode over to the nearby patch of garden, and ripped the stitched top open with her sharp iron teeth "Separate out the poppy seeds."

Tiny black seeds tumbled from the bag onto the tilled dirt, lost amid the dark soil.

Vasilisa swallowed. But she nodded again, knowing she would be trapped forever, eaten with the feast if she failed. When she failed . . . no.

She hardened her resolution. Inside her pocket, the doll squeezed her trembling hand.

A horseman in red flowing cloaks raced by the clearing, and the tendrils of dawn broke through the darkness. Vasilisa blinked, and Baba Yaga was gone.

The girl squeezed the doll back once more and began her work, only resting for a moment, well after the house was neat and the bones of the fence were polished, to give her doll some crumbs to eat and water to drink, pleading for its help. The doll, naturally, was ready.

As Vasilisa worked on Baba Yaga's feast, finding every requested herb for the stew and pushing up her sleeves to grind down the wheat berries for the bread, songbirds flew down from the trees, plucking the poppy seeds from the garden, dropping them one by one back into the burlap sack. Long before dusk, all of the tasks were done. Vasilisa found a red thread to restitch the top of the burlap sack. She embroidered her initials then her mother's, followed by tiny birds, and a line of tiny wooden dolls, sized as if to fit one inside the other, inside the next.

When Baba Yaga returned to a tidy house, a polished fence, a magnificent feast, and the bag of poppy seeds sitting charmingly beside her door, she grumbled and swore. The witch tore into her dinner, eyeing the magic lights glowing on her fence posts. Vasilisa stood taller but stayed silent, letting the witch enjoy the most complicated meal she'd ever prepared, knowing how hard she'd worked and how well she'd succeeded by the lack of crumbs left behind.

Baba Yaga barely looked at the girl when she gave Vasilisa one of the skulls from her fence. Red fire glowed within, a fire the witch promised would never go out. The smooth bone was warm in the girl's hand as she accepted the light she had requested. She willed her hands not to shake as she thanked Baba Yaga with her best manners, remembering her mother's teachings from such a long time ago.

Light emerged from the skull's empty eye sockets, eerie spotlights that seemed to blink on occasion. But Vasilisa watched her steps, around blooming white wood anemone, gnarled roots, and fallen leaves. The nighttime winds pushed her out of the depths of the forest. The entanglement of boughs overhead soon became nothing more than intermittent branches.

Her stepmother's hut soon came into view, but again, Vasilisa didn't allow her hands carrying the glowing skull to tremble. She emerged from the last of the dark, dark woods, raising her chin when she saw her stepmother and stepsisters gathered outside the front door, trying to patch their clothing by the scant light of the waxing moon.

When the three looked up, the skull in Vasilisa's hands glowed brighter. The moon hid itself behind a passing cloud, yet the clearing was suddenly full of light. A flash like lightning shot from the skull's eyes toward the three women crouched on their crooked stoop.

First fire, then dust, then they were nothing more.

As dawn emerged, Vasilisa buried the glowing skull as deep as she could within the soil of the small house's garden, knowing that the light from Baba Yaga would always hold its own wiles. When the shovel blistered her hands, she asked the doll for strength in her body and strength in her soul, and the doll told her it was already so. It had always been, and it would always be. For wickedness couldn't break dedication, nor cleverness, nor kindness, nor faith. A girl's power doesn't lie just in muscle. Its profundities lay in wait underneath.

CHAPTER EIGHT

A Donor for the Deserving

Wooden nesting dolls, also called *matryoshka,* always come to mind when thinking about Vasilisa's wooden doll. It holds her mother's strength, keeping Vasilisa strong, just as sets of matryoshka dolls are each shaped and held safe by all the others. The protection of the oldest and biggest shelters the next in line, who guards the next, and onward and onward. Vasilisa isn't a doll herself, but the wooden doll her mother gave her holds her fast and protects her, no matter what she may face.

The doll fortifies her as she transforms into the young woman ready for marriage, for in most versions of the tale, the ending includes a wedding with the son of the tsar. The doll is there with her as she digs into her own reserves to not only remain kind and respectful but to find greater bravery and ingenuity than ever before. The discipline and gumption she demonstrates in response to Baba Yaga are lessons she can carry with her forever more.

In Vasilisa's oft told tale, the magic doll is at times wooden and at others made of rag. The game of Telephone has twisted its material and form, but one particular Slavic tradition seems closely related to the fairy godmother–like doll's revered role.

A subset of the Finno-Ugric people, a population that has stretched from northern Scandinavia east to Siberia and down through central Europe for thousands of years, had—and potentially still have—a custom that may linger in the story of Vasilisa's doll. This large group once shared customs rooted in early agricultural and nomadic belief systems. The Uralic family of languages traced to this group began to split between roughly 5000 and 4000 BCE. The Permian branch of the Finno-Ugrics likely differentiated itself between approximately 2500 and 2000 BCE. The Baltic Finns had distinguished themselves by roughly 1500 BCE, and the Volga Finns began separating around 1200 BCE. However, the Nenets, descendants of a Finno-Ugric group living in southwestern Siberia, have a distinctive doll-making tradition.

The Nenets are a people living today. The modern world, its government systems, and its technology constantly encroach upon their lands and customs, but their reindeer-herding expertise, honed over thousands of years, remains in practice. Certain hand-built Nenet sleds of the present day match sleds in the archeological record for this population 8,000 years ago, which speaks to the value of tradition and steadfast preservation of that which works well.

The Nenets, understandably, do not commonly share particulars of their systems or spiritual beliefs with outsiders, but external examinations of this group may have sparked the legacy of Vasilisa's doll. Specifically, observational records note sacred dolls, which are honored with their own sleds during migrations. Only certain Nenet individuals seem to have the right to approach these dolls. Potentially related, Nenet shamans have been known to make "death dolls" of heroic figures. Certain dolls were honored and fed for long periods of time, half a century, maybe more. Note the idea of "feeding" these dolls. This practice's continuation into the present day is unclear, and as an outsider myself, I will not begin to explain any intricacies of this group. But I do know storytelling. Unique observations seize upon the human mind and imagination, and these observations weave their ways into new stories—no matter if truth, mystery, misconception, or blatant falsehood is their true origin.

We should respect the desires of a community that strives to remain detached and autonomous, and I will not attempt to discuss their traditions out of context. Nevertheless, one could understand how a traveler to these Arctic lands might come back with certain assumptions.

Is this the origin of Vasilisa's doll from her dead mother, which she treats as her own sacred relic, which she has to feed to ensure its strength and ongoing power? I cannot guarantee this tie, but an ancient tradition with an overlapping geographic footprint is certainly a clue worth considering. A similar Finno-Ugric group closer to the Balkans held beliefs about the red-capped mushrooms, as we've previously discussed—mushrooms later seized upon by Baba Yaga illustrators like Ivan Yakovlevich Biliban.

Baba Yaga continues to show hints of her origins and the traditions that have surrounded her lands in the smallest details of her stories. So many years and so many peoples have influenced this witch like no other.

In spite of everything, the word *witch* makes me stumble every time I write it. Much like the word *doll* is far short of Vasilisa's fairy godmother–like pocket companion, the term *witch* is such an oversimplification of who Baba Yaga is. Sure, the ancient old woman may threaten to boil you, bake you, or grind you up with her iron teeth. Cannibalistic rumors persist. Human bones hint at horrors. But few, if any, folktales deliver upon this threat. Food for thought, no? Or should we say lack of food with these Baba Yaga thoughts?

Who's to say the bones that make up her fence and gate were her victims or individuals she chose to cherish and preserve for other reasons entirely. Maybe much like a death doll, they are signs of honor and respect for those she helped transport to the other side of life.

Here's what do we know: this supposed witch can terrorize and torture with the best—or worst?—of world literature's villains, yet she also has a side she doesn't flaunt, a side she in many ways shares with Vasilisa's doll. No sparkling silver wand, fairy dust, or rainbows hint at the goodness of Baba Yaga, but in her own dark way, she encourages characters to be at their best, as we've seen. Pushing this further, she even works her magic for others, upon request, if properly convinced.

A motherless girl, harassed by her stepmother, gains her fire, after all. Thus, Vasilisa's doll is not the only giver of gifts and magical assistance in this story.

The extra present—if we can darkly phrase it that way—of ridding Vasilisa of her stepmother and stepsisters was just a bonus. Vasilisa had clearly made an impression, so Baba Yaga gave her something a bit extra. Horrified, Vasilisa buried the skull in her garden so it wouldn't harm anyone else, but can't you imagine Baba Yaga watching the entire scene from behind a nearby tree trunk or from her mortar far overhead, pestle in hand, ready to get moving if anyone detects her?

The old witch would be joyous that her gift worked so perfectly, although Vasilisa didn't quite agree. Yet Vasilisa came to her with a desperate desire, and Baba Yaga granted it. Why Vasilisa didn't ask her doll for such assistance, we may never know, but we do know that Baba Yaga's powers exceed all others'.

Here, again, we see the unique character of Baba Yaga amid so many other folktale sorceresses. She's not convinced by payment or bribes. She doesn't ask you to kill her enemies or quest for a secret relic far away. She doesn't beg for tricks or sacrifice. No, Baba Yaga is only a godmother figure if she deems you worthy. Worthiness and proving yourself are everything to her.

A young girl on a quest to bring a candle back to her stepmother's cottage where the last fire has gone out.

A boy born with a deformity that scares his family and neighbors away.

A young man lied to by his friends.

Baba Yaga may have once been a goddess of the earth, a symbol for the lethality and ruthlessness of the wilderness, or the personification of a plow, breaking the field to allow it to grow anew. She is a woman that possesses all the terror and destruction hiding in the darkest parts of the forest, but through her work, new promises emerge.

The young girl seeking fire earns it amid the terrifying shadows.

The boy once shunned is taught to harness his power to change the world.

The young man prospers while his former friends are trapped forever underground.

If given the chance to meet with a savage witch who could transform your world and your possibilities, would you do it? Imagine walking into the darkness of the wood, weaving forward amid vine-tangled boughs, stumbling over decaying trunks heavy with lichen, and ducking under low-limbed trees reaching out as if their bare branches were boney fingers. But "would you do it?" is only one side of the matter. Perhaps the better question is, if you dared, would she deem you worthy?

We've spoken of character building and initiation rites, but personal transformation is different from having gifts bestowed upon you. Again, this is where the name *witch* slips away. *Donor* instead comes to mind, as this term is also a character type in such tales, but this label is equally insufficient.

When meeting Baba Yaga, characters never quite know if she will help or hurt them, but the knowledge of her magic lures people toward her time and again. She has many secrets after all—secrets hard-earned over millennia—no matter whether we regard her as a medicine woman or a midwife, a naturalist recluse, or a shaman lost in time. She has gifts, but not just anyone may depart with them.

Beauty, riches, and birthright don't matter to her, and the arrogance of those who assume she will unquestioningly bestow her aid will lead to failure in their pursuits with gruesome results. If you've heard complaints about how "kids these days" feel so entitled, Baba Yaga would likely snort and nod her boney neck in agreement, especially after her hundreds of years dealing with young men and women sneaking into her forest sanctuary.

Privilege is not a reality for her. Life circumstances mean nothing. What determines worthiness to Baba Yaga is how you act.

Not what you have.

Not what you say.

And clever tricks will backfire, I promise you. Oh, even Yvashka's honey plot fails eventually.

Nevertheless, if you are respectful and brave, if you are smart and good-hearted, Baba Yaga will reward you. We'll add being a hard worker into the mix too. Only someone not afraid to push up their sleeves and get the necessary work done will earn her satisfaction. She will be grumpy, stubborn, and horrific, but she will give you what you desperately need. She might toss in a bonus present, if you want it or not.

What, in the end, is the role served by a fairytale or folktale villain? They are there to scare us, to teach us to follow the right and safe path, to remind us of the danger of strangers and the darkness of the unknown. Villains are there to give us an accessible way to confront the darkness of the world. They keep us in balance, as happy-go-lucky children skipping under the dappled sunshine at the edge of the wood or as adults steadfastly questing for our dreams to come true.

"Donor" character types have their unique roles too. They remind us of hope in any circumstance and that the dreams we imagine can become a reality if we focus our thoughts and intentions. Princess Aurora, also known as "Sleeping Beauty," has the three good fairies who bestow gifts upon her and protect her. Cinderella has her fairy godmother. But where does Baba Yaga fit amid these categorizations?

The donor role sometimes overlaps with a "trickster" character type, but rarely with a villain. We see tricksters across world mythologies. They hold secrets the protagonists need, and they don't give up their knowledge easily. They create impediments in a hero's journey and break conventional social rules. Does this sound familiar? From Loki to Kaggen to

Coyote to Puck, we're familiar with these troublesome and mischievous characters, but they usually don't threaten death, Marvel Universe aside.

Here Baba Yaga, once again, stands alone against her contemporaries, just as she once stood alone in the table in Mikhail W. Lomonosov's 1755 *Russian Grammar*. She is not a perpetual trickster. She is not a pure villain. She is not a benevolent donor holding fast to this role and this role alone.

The old witch, if we dare to name her as such, keeps our expectations for happily ever after in check. She reminds us to be on our guard, to be our best self, and to dream our dreams. Yet she also ensures we know that wishes are not granted by the blessing of a guardian angel or a desperate yearning with fingers crossed. True heroes and heroines have to make their own desires come to life, even when trickster types keep them on their toes.

Vasilisa may indeed resemble Cinderella in many ways, but when Baba Yaga and the many cultural traditions that surround her are twisted into the tale, she will defy everything we think we know. Donors can be dolls or ancient witches, after all. And what dreams may come will not be anything you expected.

9

"BABA YAGA & THE KINDHEARTED GIRL"

he feeling is well-known: you meet someone familiar in a way you can't quite name. You've never seen them before; you're sure of it. But something about them stirs a trepidation that quivers down every vertebra of your spine, one by one. Illogical apprehension squeezes the breath from your lungs before words have any hope of escaping.

Natasha's new stepmother troubled her insides in just such a way. The woman was achingly familiar, but a mind can play tricks. Natasha's house had been hers and her father's alone for years now. But here was a stepmother, holding out an empty spool with the last wisp of thread pinched between her oddly recognizable fingers.

"Go to my sister for more." Her stepmother's demand ricocheted against the walls before smacking the girl across the cheek—if such a scene could be so, though it certainly couldn't.

"I have more thread, stepmother." Natasha turned to fetch her sewing box, biting her lip against the improbable pain. "I believe I have precisely that shade—"

"This thread is special," the new but familiar woman interjected. "Only my sister has more. Go to her. She is now your auntie, after all."

Natasha put a hand to the wall beside her. Her cheek still stung.

"I haven't met my new aunt." She traced her fingers along the grain of wood, stopping at the window frame to look out. Shadows stretched. Daylight faded. Her head ached.

"Oh, but she lives in a hut in the woods, not so close, but not so far." Her voice was almost sweet now. Had it all been Natasha's imagination? "Toward the faraway kingdom," the woman continued, raising a thick, wild brow.

Natasha's heart snagged on the words, not knowing how long the journey could be. She offered her own threads again, her plentiful spools and bobbins, but her new stepmother shook her head, pointing her chin and sharp nose toward the door.

Natasha tied back her hair with her favorite ribbon, collected a snack in her handkerchief, and left the house that once had been hers and her father's alone. The sun was low. Shadows stretched and wove themselves thicker and thicker. Natasha tripped on an old oil can on the road. Catching herself, she guessed if something stood in her path, it must be there for a reason. She picked it up and brought it along.

Natasha wandered as confidently as she dared, wishing her father knew of the errand she'd been sent upon, wishing she had said something to someone, to anyone.

A thorn-strangled tree reached its branches like claws across the thin dirt road before her. Natasha swept a fallen stick across its choked limbs to disentangle the worst of the barbed creepers. Then, with nothing better coming to mind, she pulled the ribbon from her hair to fasten back the remaining barricade.

Footsteps of wolves padded beside her in the inky darkness beyond the trail. Birds of prey swooped through the air so fast they were gone before she turned their way—absent but for the terrified shrieks and squeaks of their prey. A gate appeared in the murky darkness, swaying open and shut, open and shut, its hinges whining with the movement. But surely this was why she found the oil.

Natasha oiled the squeaky hinges until the gate fell silent, but when she took her first step through, the house that stood before her made her gasp. She dropped the can. It clanged to the ground, dribbling black liquid into a growing puddle next to her shoes, but she couldn't give the mess her attention. The little hut spun around and around, never stopping, never ceasing, making her dizzy, though she couldn't look away.

Grasping the familiarity of the woman her father had married, Natasha knew the words she needed. Her new stepmother was sister to Baba Yaga, and this was the old witch's house.

Natasha pressed her lips together as a mouse scuttled by. A cat slunk through the shadows then crouched low in a patch of dead feathergrass. Its eyes held fast to her. She forced out the words from all the stories:

Little hut, little hut,
Turn your back to the forest and your front toward me.

The hut stopped spinning, and its door swung open. The resemblance to her stepmother was clear in the woman who now appeared—the long sharp nose, the beady eyes, and the scrawny, chicken bone neck.

"Dearest Auntie?" Natasha's voice cracked.

"Niece," Baba Yaga began, eyeing the girl up and down before looking back to the house behind her. "I have more thread for my sister, but first you must stay and be of assistance to me."

Natasha's hair flew in her face as a new cold breeze blew against her. A breeze or the beating of owl wings. No ribbon remained to hold her locks back. She nodded, suddenly certain she hadn't mentioned the thread.

"First, take a bath, for you are filthy. Then I need your help with my weaving and . . . and with putting something rather large in my oven." Baba Yaga reached to the dirt-patched grass where a sieve lay forgotten. "You can fill up the tub with this. The well is there." She pointed with her chin, exactly as her sister had, handing over the metal sieve with its countless holes before disappearing inside.

Natasha swallowed again, pushing her messy hair back out of her face. At least her head ached less than it had before. She walked over to the well, drew up a bucket of water, and dipped the sieve inside. The water trickled straight through.

The cat wove against Natasha's legs, looking up to her with amber eyes. She reached into her pocket and gave the skinny creature some of the meat she had brought in her handkerchief. The cat gobbled it up quickly, as an idea struck her. She pulled massive leaves from a nearby poplar tree, layering them one upon the other upon the next until she created a thick base to the sieve. She dipped it once again into the bucket, using her other hand to hold the leaves in place, then lifted it. The water held. She moved to the tub as quickly as she could and found she could fill it quite well.

After she was clean, she returned to the old witch who sat at her loom. Natasha listened to her orders before taking over the work.

"Of course, Auntie," she whispered, wishing there were at least windows in the small wooden hut. Nearby candles flickered as she moved the pedals as instructed, the threads weaving neatly, precisely as she was shown, for Natasha had always been a quick study.

The cat brushed up against her legs again, its soft mew somehow emerging in a language she recognized.

"If I press the pedals," the thin cat began, "the witch will hear the clickity clack, clickity clack. She will think you are still weaving." Its wide amber eyes met her own. "She is tending the garden. Go. You can run out of the house and out the gate on the other side."

Natasha put a hand to the rough wooden wall of the small, confined hut. She took in a breath, nodding as she released it.

"Thank you, cat," she whispered, but the cat didn't answer. It only jumped into place, batting at the loose thread twice, before resuming the rhythm of her clickity clack, clickity clack.

Natasha ran as silently as she could, out of the hut, out of the gate, and down the path in the direction away from the faraway kingdom.

The cat, meanwhile, was not as quick a study as Natasha. When Baba Yaga returned, she found the thin creature surrounded by a tangle, thread in its teeth and some in its claws. Nonetheless, it continued on as best it could with the clickity clack, clickity clack.

"What are you doing?" Baba Yaga shrieked.

"Natasha gave me delicious meat," the cat answered. "You've never given me more than bones."

The witch threw the forgotten sieve at the cat before clomping out the hut's door.

"Why didn't you squeak to warn me?" the old witch demanded of the gate.

"The kind girl oiled my hinges, something you have never done," answered the gate, swinging silently and proudly in the breeze.

Baba Yaga lumbered onward, down the path, around the bend until the tangled bramble came into sight.

"You!" she screamed at the bramble tree. "You were supposed to block the path, preventing anyone's travels."

"But the kind girl tied me up with a beautiful ribbon," the tree answered, its blue bow tilting toward the witch as a bird landed nearby. "You have never given me any gifts."

Baba Yaga yanked out the ribbon. The tree branch released and struck her in the face, causing the old witch to whirl into a frenzy, a frenzy that forgot all about Natasha, who had long forgotten about the thread.

CHAPTER NINE

Domestic Precision in a Chicken-Legged Hut

Industrious heroines and their work within Baba Yaga's home deserve our attention, as does the strange hut itself. How we exist amid challenging circumstances says so much about who we are, because challenges will always arise. Needless to say, Baba Yaga answers her own trials and severe circumstances with two solutions: first, her one-of-a-kind chicken-legged hut and second, recruiting—or shall we say kidnapping—girls to assist with the workload of an otherwise self-sufficient witch in the forest.

Kidnapping may be too strong of a word. She certainly kidnapped Marusia, but Vasilisa and Natasha both came to her. These two young women were heroes, of a kind, questing on a mission. Vasilisa came for light and Natasha for thread.

They both sought out Baba Yaga's chicken-legged hut amid the harsh conditions in their own lives, and they found temporary refuge there. Some houses protect from the weather. Magical houses on skinny chicken legs with claws that occasionally scratch the undergrowth offer different kinds of sanctuary. Absurdism meets the natural world, and that's where fairytales and folktales thrive.

As a structure, the chicken hut is famous for repositioning itself. Often hard to find within the darkest parts of the forest, it moves from place to place to avoid detection. If you do discover its location, the house can stretch itself up and fling dirt and stones in your direction, its nonsensical feathers also releasing into the air. However, a certain magical phrase will encourage the house to turn toward a knowing visitor, no matter if Baba Yaga approves or not.

The words are fairly consistent over the many tales:

> *Little hut, little hut,*
> *Turn your back to the forest and your front toward me.*

Shall we call it an obedient little chicken? Does such a creature exist? Hedgehogs, I do know to a certain degree. Chickens, I can't say that I do.

Whether the house is well trained or another part of Baba Yaga's magic is at play is unclear. But with this spell, if we dare to call it such, the heroine finds herself face-to-face with the front door.

In my version of Natasha's story, I played with the legacy in which the hut constantly spins and only these words will stop its revolving. Other tales claim the hut turns depending on the season or the time of day. Sometimes her chicken-legged hut has one leg, though usually two. I've heard it with four but never three in my awareness. Some stories claim "fowl's feet," neglecting to clarify further, but goat's feet too are mentioned in some regions. A rooster is known to occasionally sprout from the roof, but like Baba Yaga's bear claw hands and ogress qualities, this squawking head appears only rarely.

In the most popular versions, Baba Yaga's hut looks as you'd expect a cottage in the woods might—that is, until it shifts and moves. Scrawny but mighty scaled-skin legs reveal themselves underneath, vestiges from the Jurassic or a farmer's strangest dreams.

The moment you meet the "villain" in any folktale is pivotal, but merely approaching this strange house elevates the tension and magic. Natasha gasps. Audiences have for centuries. Forget ominous lairs and castles; this hut is one of a kind. Windowless and unsteady, raised above the ground, this home exists not only in the darkness of the forest, but also in the darkness between death and slumber, the realms of unconsciousness.

Older traditions give a similar hut to a magical bear or to the mischievous leshy, tricksters of the forest, but before the first telling of its chicken legs came the inspirations for the story. Two ancient practices could have had their own influence on the origins of this hut.

A central Russian population known as the Mordvins—and specifically a subset of this group known as the Moksha—once had a sacred burial practice for revered shamans that evokes a familiar image. After death, a wooden coffin was constructed and raised up on stilts, allowing the deceased individual to exist between the sky and the earth, between the planes of life and death, not returning the body to the dirt from whence it came.

When we ponder Baba Yaga's windowless hut and the occasional tales of her body so massive inside that she fills the full expanse, the idea of a coffin is not so far removed. Her nose scrapes the roof. Her feet extend into the far corners. She's suddenly not a giantess but a mere human enclosed in her final resting place. She too inhabits the space between life and death, between human society as we know it and the faraway kingdom.

Now, consider coming upon such a coffin on stilts deep within the forest. Sunlight falls in only the rarest patches, muddling the clarity of the spruce, elm, and ash around you. The leaves rustle in the wind. The forest smells alive. Then you see it, something ahead, something illogical, and a possibility you've never conceived of before snags your imagination.

The additional benefit of a raised coffin is that the revered one inside would not be bothered by the scavengers of the forest. You could argue so many individuals approach Baba Yaga in her tales like scavengers. People seek her out, wanting to steal her magic or to force her to grant them something. But her house lifts her up and protects her. It stretches itself high on its fowl's legs, turning so the door cannot be found.

But then, no door would be found in a raised coffin, no matter how many times one might circle it. Or is it the wisdom of the dead playing

tricks? Her strange house protects her and her otherworldly knowledge like the shaman's coffins of old. Thus, the ancient Moksha ritual has transfigured into folktale form. But once again, no single ritual is ever the totality of Baba Yaga's birthright.

A different structure on stilts also plays into the chicken-legged hut's possibilities. Built upon tree stumps, Siberian food storage houses held frozen or dried meat far above the ground to keep the food safe from animals. Remember how Yvashka with the Bear's Ear stumbled upon an abandoned house with shelves full of food? The connection seems quite clear. Plus, one translation difference in the Old Russian may be interpreted as a house upon "smoked legs" rather than "chicken legs," but mistranslations like these are where stories are born. Consider cut tree stumps, blackened by fire to keep them from rotting, all the same standing strong. Where their trunks meet the earth, their gnarled roots spread, digging into the soil. Imagine the visual differences between chicken legs with their taloned feet and such charred tree trunks, held strong by their root systems barely visible above the ground. Once again, we have plausible theories albeit no definitive answers. So goes the existence of Baba Yaga.

Every twist of the tales derives from somewhere. Human imagination is a power beyond the conceivable; however, Baba Yaga's nomadic homestead also echoes historical realities archeologists and historians explore as well. As we've discussed, roughly seven thousand years ago, the people of Trypillia, potentially the first complex civilization in Europe, worshipped a female deity, but beyond their sophisticated pottery, fired in advanced kilns, and their population centers that were known to accommodate up to 15,000 people, they shifted their agriculture fields outside of their cities. These farming settlements moved from place to place, for they understood the value of alternating the soil surrounding their seeds and the freshness of the land underneath their feet. A home that can move from place to place has its advantages. Doesn't Baba Yaga know this same truth well? Why we know so little of Trypillia is a rabbit hole to dive down on another occasion—curiouser and curiouser—but all signs point to the distant past's echoes still reverberating oh so faintly in our modern ears.

In nearby regions, thousands of years later, the Scythians roamed these lands, inhabiting the steppes of the northern Black Sea region from the seventh century BCE and having a presence in Slavic regions, particularly in Crimea, through the second century of the Common Era. These were a true nomadic people, known to wander quite like Baba Yaga's hut. The Scythians were known for their horsemanship and their skill in battle, but they, too, had a goddess of the home and hearth, no matter if that home and hearth was less fixed in its geographic positioning. Her name was Tabiti—although some scholars have suggested different appellations, including "Ma," "Aga," or fascinatingly even "Yaga." For the Scythians, she was guardian of the animals, the keeper of fire, and protectress of the home. Some legends say that when Tabiti's horse-riding Scythians met the end of their great reign over the steppes, she retreated into the woods where she grew old and forgotten. Echoes of familiar tales appear again and again, no?

Final resting places and food storage houses on stilts, ancient worship and great respect for women, homes not constrained to one location, and a deep understanding of animals and the natural world, which allows for our collective prosperity and survival—such notions could easily transform generation by generation, across steppes and plains and mountains, into the tales we know today.

The aged witch has her wrinkles, her yellowed skin the shade of mushrooms, and her white hair as rebellious and untamed as she is. Baba Yaga is a woman with a complex history, but she also uses whatever she has to make ends meet. Perhaps this includes scrawny chicken feet, the remains left untouched in the kitchen after the great feast has been prepared. Waste not, want not. Why not add them to her hut for the sake of mobility?

But let's weave all these connections together, wrapping them like a special silver thread around a wooden bobbin, holding fast everything we've come to know. Her chicken-footed house has its surprises, but the precision work within it also defies all expectations.

When Baba Yaga encounters strong female protagonists, she delights in their possibilities—and not solely as individuals primed for transformation into the masters of "women's work" that they will become. No, the to-do list inside her chicken-legged hut is more than a matter of chores amid harsh conditions. The young women who enter Baba Yaga's home as anything other than meals also undergo studies in three exacting disciplines: purification, preparation, and precision.

In nearly all stories when someone is invited into Baba Yaga's chicken-legged hut, one of the first commands Baba Yaga gives is for her visitor to take a bath. The jarring "Russian scent" of her guests, so strong to the old witch's sensitive long nose, could be the inspiration for such requests, but consider too that bathing is also a purification ritual. The first challenge may include filling the bathtub with a sieve, an impossible task to all but the clever who find their ways, or the bath may be drawn by a servant, who is another trapped girl, an animal, or a disconnected pair of hands scrambling about to do Baba Yaga's bidding. No matter its specifics, the baptism into the faith of her house is repeatedly the beginning of Baba Yaga's training.

The world is covered in filth, grime, and failings that desperately need to be scrubbed away, after all. Cleanliness's relation to godliness is a matter of debate, but washing off the dust of our past enables a fresh start. Thus, Baba Yaga's hut allows for a cleansing bath and renewal. Wherever you have been and whatever you have been before, if you are invited inside and not directly into her oven, you have proven yourself worthy of a reviving.

Although if you fail at your next tasks, the old witch may always argue that cleaner bodies make for more delicious meals.

This purification is then followed by preparation, essential for any who seek to change themselves or the messy world around them. The fall of night can bring its terrors. The extremes of the weather can threaten our very existence. Folktales allow us to confront antagonists so we are ready to meet anything that may rise up against us in our own lives, even if it is not a witch's curse or black geese in the sky.

The seasons can be as unforgiving as Baba Yaga's tempers, challenging the continuation of life itself if not for your preparation, diligence, and determination. Baba Yaga's hut may be on the border of "the far-away kingdom," but think about the climate in Russia, Ukraine, Poland, Belarus, Latvia, and the many countries where Baba Yaga tales originated. The capacity of the cold in many of these places can be ruthless. Those of us with well-built roofs over our heads and easy access to heat and air-conditioning might do well to remember that nature challenges indiscriminately. As we face climate changes in our modern-day lives, we may well be reminded to pay attention.

Meanwhile, in the world of folktales, Natasha oiled rusty hinges and tied back tangled vines from the road, putting the world she found into better order than before. She didn't realize she was preparing these paths for her own escape. However, isn't preparation what always leads us to our best results?

Furthermore, the precision of Natasha's work made all the difference. Tying back the last of the thorns with the ribbon from her hair didn't just address the problem; it fully resolved it. Layering leaves within the sieve allowed for the well-water to fill the bath. Being a quick study at the loom to please Baba Yaga allowed for her independence amid the ongoing clickity clack, clickity clack.

Vasilisa too needed to find her most meticulous nature as she scrubbed the bones of Baba Yaga's fence, prepared a colossal feast, and sorted poppy seeds from flecks of black soil—although, once again, clever thinking and the assistance of those she was kind to made all the difference.

Preparation and precision both are essential in daily life. The battle for clean homes continues after all, a less examined but oh-so-real tale as old as time. In life, chaos and disorder can lurk around every corner, but at least within our homes, we can strive to win the fight. Purification, preparation, precision. Thus, Baba Yaga's chores are less tedious and more profound. Hero's quests come in many forms. Pursuits need not be epic to be grand.

The moral is not merely to work hard, be the best cook, and the best keeper of the house to find a good husband. Stories reflect the eras of their birth, yet a greater theme persists above these once-standard lessons in a girl's education. The larger takeaway is that the imperfect—no matter what it may be—needs to be acknowledged and examined, especially when the details cannot be resolved in a single stroke of magic. Baba Yaga makes the young protagonists who come to her work to empower the situation they find themselves in. Not all of us have the magic touch, but we are all full of endless possibilities, wherever we find ourselves. Natasha, Vasilisa, and so many more remind us of this.

Forest animals may not come to our beck and call to help us pluck the poppy seeds from the dirt or distract our enemy with the hope of botanical remedies for youthful skin, but possibilities always remain. Camaraderie lingers in the blink of a familiar cat. We have within us the answers to the most overwhelming messes if we dare to try. Not to say our houses will remain clean, but we can strive on all the same.

Still, one specific task is almost always on Baba Yaga's chore list. Cooking, we must remember, is more than a duty; at its essence, meal preparation is the creation of sustenance for a life to have the energy to go on. These heroines have great power within their grasp when their daily work is reexamined from this perspective. Ancient traditions are once again in play, particularly when examining the old witch's oven.

Ancient shrine models found in Popudnia, a village in western Ukraine, depict figurines grinding grain, preparing dough, and baking bread. Such foods were dedicated to a goddess, presumably of the hearth. Scholars argue that baking rituals linked to sacred practices go back to the Neolithic period. Preparation and precision in the creation of life's sustenance were a holy matter.

The goddess known as Mokosh had similar connection. While closely associated with cooking, knitting, wool-spinning, crocheting, weaving, laundry, and washing, she is not a goddess of housework. Remember, she had a statue raised to her in the year 980 in Kiev, as a goddess of creation.

Ovens have also had an association with not only baked bread but the womb itself for millennia. We are given an enclosed, protected space for growth, for transformation—a space historically tended by the women of the household. This link lingers in Baba Yaga's stories. Sure, the old witch's oven could be a hellish punishment if you do not live up to Baba Yaga's strict standards, but at the center of her tiny hut, the oven also remains a symbol of rebirth, a symbol of the earth's gifts (grain) transformed into nourishment. A goddess of creation and transformation is thus clearly linked with a goddess of the hearth and the sacred but everyday routines of living.

When Baba Yaga demands work in her chicken-legged hut, she commands respect for ancestral traditions and one's own role as a change maker. Endless work remains. The discipline required for tidying our immediate surroundings can match the same determined approach on a greater scale—if we dare to take on the mess.

Homes fall into disorder, and that's okay. We've all been there. I know my home can stray far from perfection. But rooms can be dusted, scrubbed, and spit-polished to a shine. Transformations come from the cleaning of our spaces and our souls. We brush off the dirt and dust, going back to the core of who we can be, remembering what that looks like under the layers of grime that life lays down upon us.

What if we kept our hands busy with deeds that need doing rather than endless scrolling on screens? Baba Yaga would see her surroundings and create a to-do list. The protagonists she invites into her house would do the same.

Her chicken-footed hut, inspired by history and imagination alike, in no way ties her down. Rather, the magic hut instills a sense of possibility. When similarly bound to the confines of necessary domesticity, we could ask Baba Yaga's familiar question: are you here to do deeds or run from them? Hero's quests take many forms. What will yours look like today?

10

"THE PURSUIT
of THE FIREBIRD"

he knock on the door never comes when you're expecting it. As for Baba Yaga, she had just sent a raven to the roof to keep watch over the night. She had scarcely closed her eyes. Then a howl accompanied the knocking.

Prince Ivan Tsarovich had a firebird's feather in one hand, the golden reins of a golden-maned horse in the other, and a jaw clenched with all the bravery he could muster.

"Good evening, dear grandmother."

Baba Yaga lifted her pointy chin at this.

"I am told you know where we can find Koscheii the Deathless." Prince Ivan squared his shoulders, standing as tall as he could, waiting for her next move. But she kept every inch of herself still. A wolf flexed its muscles at the prince's side.

"Koscheii has a princess trapped," Ivan continued, clearly forcing himself to hold her eyes. "Her name is Helena, and I will be killed if I can't find her."

The wolf bared its teeth and growled a vibration so deep she doubted human ears could hear the sound. Baba Yaga didn't shift her weight from one boney leg to another. Her raven called overhead. And did she nod? Or was that just the wind in her scraggly hair mimicking the dance of the pussy willow leaves around them?

"Dear grandmother," the third son of the tsar pressed on. She did love his desperation. And his respect. "Can you help? I will do anything—"

She lifted her hand, waving away the suggestion. The raven took flight, its wings slicing through the charcoal darkness of the starless night. She would invite this young prince inside her hut. She'd feed him well and grant the prince's request. Koscheii likely deserved it anyhow, the old immortal bastard. The prince would free the captive princess and return her to her kingdom, only to win her hand. He would return the golden-maned horse to the next realm's king who would allow him to live to return the firebird with its golden flame feathers to his own father, so the bird would stop stealing the tsar's golden apples and all would be well.

All would be well, that is, until Prince Ivan's brothers killed him, which Baba Yaga knew was still coming. Knowing so much gave her headaches sometimes. But the raven would deliver the waters of mending, which would stitch together his fragmented body, and the waters of life would stir breath in his lungs and a pulse in his heart once again. She'd already sent the raven on his way, allowing all to be well. Because every so often, all should be well.

Just as Ivan knew that firebirds almost always meant trouble and that daring to pick up a feather was certainly always the start of a quest, Baba Yaga knew that answering a knock at the door in the middle of the night in the deepest part of the woods was never a simple endeavor. Sometimes it came with a gift of fresh fruit or newly baked bread. Other times, it came with rants and torches. Yet an old woman hidden away from the world tried to do what she could, especially when the world dared to ask nicely.

CHAPTER TEN

Rebellions & Unlikely Inspirations

Witches are frequently stuck in their plotlines, but Baba Yaga doesn't fit into the simple constraints of a "witch." Under the pussy willow trees or across a peat bog, dotted with marsh cinquefoil and bogbean, she stretches the bounds of being a villain. Familiar plotlines arise, but in her multiplicity over centuries, we see a more complex story emerge from the muck-stained darkness.

Firebird narratives are plentiful in Slavic folklore, but Baba Yaga's place in this particular one presents a glimpse of something little appreciated in other tales. Yes, Vasilisa goes to her for fire, and Natasha goes to her for thread; but Ivan seeks out Baba Yaga for her knowledge of the otherworldly. She is on her own amid the darkest realms of the forest. Our hero knows she may well deny him. She may well kill him. Her obstinacy and sense of self-protection are well known.

Yet audiences may not realize the willows that surround her also produce branches incorporated into Palm Sunday services in a region where palms are not native. They are holy, only not. Pussy willow cores additionally produce the wood for crafting bandura, a stringed instrument famous for ballads and folk songs. Early forms of bandura, called kobza, lent their names to the Ukrainian minstrels famous for their tales, the kobzars.

Secrets in the wood, secrets in the forest. Not even the waters of mending could stitch together all the inspirations, though I will continue to try. Nonetheless, with odds against him and his wolf at his side,

Prince Ivan understands the importance of starting with the respect Baba Yaga deserves. Villain she may sometimes be, but her rebellious nature emboldens her birthright.

Protagonists know Baba Yaga's power doesn't come from her beauty or wealth or relationships with men—typical places a woman might find power in fairytales. Nor is her authority bound only to magic. Instead, her self-sufficiency, stubbornness, and rejection of numerous social standards recasts her from witch or crone to unlikely inspiration, a renegade against external expectations. Simple witches are perfect for Saturday morning cartoons—in a day when Saturday morning cartoons were their own tradition—however, Baba Yaga's life lessons don't end with "be good or the old witch of the woods will eat you." As her audiences grow and mature, they face new struggles in life. Baba Yaga has her own defiant advice here too.

But first, a question: have you ever noticed not only how Baba Yaga exists deep in the woods, but how she also truly exists on her own? No animals are her "familiars," nor are any her captives. The cats that appear have no deep ties to the old witch. The mice, bees, dogs, and lions that arise make their own choices, considering Baba Yaga's wrath but not greatly fearful of repercussions. Neither the black geese nor the occasional ravens that do her hunting are bound to her when their favor is done. They merely exist in the same place, taking care of themselves the best they can, exactly as Baba Yaga does herself.

Across history, how many women have needed a guardian or a husband to take care of them? Actually, stop. Don't try to answer that question. Baba Yaga would cackle at the thought. Or would it be beyond a cackle? Would she start warming her oven for the soul who suggested any hint of female incapability?

Empowering fight songs echo across modern popular landscapes, but in her own way, Baba Yaga has always added her own voice to this conversation. Alone in the woods, amid the silver fir and ancient beech, she has her own passions that drive her daily efforts, although her work largely remains "off-screen" amid a different hero or heroine's story. She doesn't need the spotlight. She's disciplined and unperturbed by those who live differently, as long as they allow her to live her life too. Remember, in most tales, no confrontation arises unless characters seek her out and disturb her.

She is there to hear the secrets whispered into a hole in the earth. She is a goddess revered, receiving visitors with the freshest smelling bread, fruit, and meat sacrifices in return for promises of health and safety. She is the worst force of the winter wind and ice. She is the rebirth of the spring, when the earth has been shredded by a plow and is ready for its next chapter to begin. She is waiting with fire and thread and secrets.

As she serves her role in initiation rites and the preparation for young women, as we've discussed, she enables these heroines to thrive in the world where they find themselves. The old witch and goddess understands the expectations cast upon them. In such a place, cleanliness, order, and meticulousness are indeed routes to finding a successful marriage. Thus, she acknowledges the formulas of the societies around her. But, simultaneously, she is almost always fascinatingly single, a defiance in its own right.

In rare stories, Koscheii the Deathless appears as her husband, but this marriage lends itself to storytellers' desires to create order and balance, even in folktales. If you have an old witch, surely, she'll be married to an old wizard, no? Oh, world, your matchmaking tendencies don't make for happily-ever-afters as frequently as you seem to think they do. Be that as it may, I do love that in these stories, Baba Yaga usually remains the more powerful of the two.

Timeworn sources have also hinted that Baba Yaga was once the fiancée of the Slavic fire god, Svarog. In this narrative, she abandons him before the wedding to go to the forest, giving up her goddess status to embrace the secret possibilities of the natural world. She decides she'd rather create ointments and elixirs to help humanity than marry a god. Thus, she flees the life thrust upon her and instead learns to communicate with the plants and animals and also to act as the guardian over the passage to the world of the dead. Doesn't this sound intriguingly familiar? She had her mission, her calling, and no social conventions were going to distract her from it. When you know your purpose for living, expectations be damned, sometimes, you've just got to go for it—at least, that's her argument.

Baba Yaga's dogged determination is at the root of her independence, and that drive is as powerful as any magic she may brew—though let us remember that her "magic" more frequently originates from nature's secrets than spell books. As we will see, she's known to go to a blacksmith for assistance when needed—perhaps an old reference to the once jilted fiancé god of fire, passed down in a game of Telephone until his role is humanized and diminished.

As an aged, determined woman, Baba Yaga seeks out the flower that can give her youth, because she cannot create such an elixir on her own. She finds sorcery within her mortar and pestle as women have done for centuries—mixing ingredients for supper, grinding grain, and making medicine. Everyday alchemy amid everyday scenes. Sure, her mortar happens to also be huge and have the ability to take flight, but that's the magic of storytelling.

Understanding her passions, Baba Yaga is also unafraid of saying no. May we all have such power in our lives. Call it obstinance or inflexibility, but her stubbornness has its own goals:

- Scaring people into being a better version of themselves? She's absolutely on it.

- Bolstering underestimated girls? Oh, she's there to mentor them.

- Thwarting overconfident young men setting out to steal her home, her food, and her liberated way of living? They'll answer with a pound of flesh, if not more. Sorry, Shakespeare. The idea did not begin with you.

Every student who studies literature is familiar with those authors considered among the canon of greats. William Shakespeare, for sure; Leo Tolstoy too is among these well-known names. Tolstoy's *Anna Karenina* became my favorite novel when I was introduced to it at the age of seventeen, not because of its Eastern European attitudes or literary weight, but because of the complexities of Anna Karenina herself. She too was a woman full of both the admirable and the reprehensible. She created her own definitions for living, with rebellions I couldn't conceive of at her core. Reading her story provoked questions about the nature of social conventions, roles in family life, compassion, judgment, and the evolving existence of humanity, and as someone who dreamed of becoming a writer, I was simultaneously awed and inspired. Only years later did I make the connection between my captivation with Anna Karenina and my enthrallment with Baba Yaga. When I realized that Tolstoy's grandfather had hired a master of Slavic folktales to tell young Leo bedtime stories, the connection became richer.

Baba Yaga, the Firebird, and Koscheii the Deathless were among the characters young Tolstoy knew well. They've been called his first literary influences. Were the complexities of Anna Karenina born of a rebellious yet inspiring ancient Slavic witch?

Forget the black geese sent for naughty children. Baba Yaga's emotions flare then settle. Then she keeps, determinedly, carrying on with her work. Storytellers can entertain. They can inspire. They can provoke new questions for audiences to explore. As for this ancient witch's motivations, haven't we all had moments when we have been horrified by happenings around us? When Baba Yaga responds by trying to scare the world into being a better place, we can't completely blame her. No one can control everything, but in her tales, she controls what she can. She continues as a threat, knowing that if her measures fail, the true darkness of the world will take a worse bite. She continues *to do what she can, because someone has got to.*

This isn't to say that Baba Yaga rebels against every standard of etiquette. She stands firmly behind some matters of decency. For example, if a hungry stranger comes to her door and respectfully asks for help or food, she will stop what she is doing to answer and feed them every time. Neither Ivan's wolf nor the firebird feather force Baba Yaga's assistance in finding Koscheii. Simple decency and hospitality for those truly in need remain important to her in the majority of her stories.

In these ways, she shows her ancient roots, giving us a glimpse of a past goddess in her old age, hiding away from the world but wanting to nurture it in spite of everything. She could be the runaway fiancée of Svarog, a wild soul unfettered by society's conventions yet constantly caring for humanity's well-being. She is a *baba*, a grandmother, taking care of her family above all else, with the fierceness inside that's unconstrained. Shall we say, "go, granny, go"? Shall we debate our own fierceness, capabilities, and compassion for others, knowing some rules are justifiably broken?

Undeniably, some matters of decorum truly aren't worth her time. When Baba Yaga's hungry, she can eat a feast enough for twelve men in one sitting, relishing every last morsel and chewing on the bones when she's done. But wouldn't we rather have her feast on those bones than on our own?

The power of stories that stir both minds and hearts makes us reconsider our surroundings. Who we have been, who we are, and who we will be seep between the lines—and those that recognize the supremacy of certain narratives seize upon them.

Ivan the Terrible, the first tsar of Russia, crowned in 1547, is said to have had three blind storytellers that each took their turns telling him a folktale before he went to sleep. Centuries later in the 1800s, advertisements for storytellers filled Russian newspapers as they sought the popular job of tellers of tales, precisely like the man hired by Leo Tolstoy's grandfather.

But the storytellers themselves were not always held in such high esteem. In Ukraine, the kobzars were traveling storytellers and kobza players, with instruments often made from the same pussy willow wood that graced Baba Yaga's tales. These minstrels and poets had their origins in the Middle Ages, sharing the histories of generations within their songs. Their epic ballads were known as *duma*, and for hundreds of years, they had their role as news carriers and preservationists of culture. However, beginning in the 1800s, the kobzars were severely persecuted and regulated for expressing too many nationalistic sentiments. The stories themselves were seen as rebellions. In 1931, hundreds of kobzars, the last of their tradition, were called to gather at a storytelling convention, and there, they were murdered by mass executions ordered by Stalin himself. Well-considered words and well-told stories have a lot of power. The biggest rebellion can be continuing to seek them out. We must learn from what remains.

Baba Yaga is nothing but a folktale character, but she is the epitome of Slavic storytelling's history: hope, pride, endurance, agitation, horror, and rebirth in the spring. Baba Yaga's independence, stubbornness, and rejection of expectations give us so much to reconsider.

Witches may be stuck in their plotlines, but Baba Yaga reminds us how well-conceived dissent has its place. A character discounted as a witch can also be the hero of the tales. Tsars and kings may force princes on deadly quests, but political leaders aren't the only ones who can initiate great pursuits and wield great powers. No offense to Ivan and his firebird, but unlikely inspirations can be the mightiest ones.

11

"IVAN & THE MAIDEN TSAR"

ave you ever woken up to fog so dense the wind whooshing through the leaves of the trees could actually be the gentle roll of the sea, and your lingering dreams haven't allowed you to remember where you are? A fog so dense it muddles your mind as well as your vision? A shroud falls upon you then, enticing you back to sleep, lulling you into complacence, and dulling any desire to stretch your limbs and begin another laborious day.

Ivan, the merchant's son, woke up to such a fog. He saw nothing but colorlessness out his bedroom window. A dried and twisted spider rested on the sill, a creature who had hatched nearby, built its webs in his bedroom, and never ventured forth to meet sea or sky.

His stepmother's skirts rustled in another room. Out the window, dawn fought on against the haze. A shape appeared far off on the horizon. Ivan squinted, imagining his tutor's reprimand at his imagination. But the shape grew. The fog burned off with the brightening rays of the sun. Waves crashed upon the rocks. A ship he'd never before seen sailed toward them.

After flicking the spider out into the fresh air, Ivan dressed and readied for the day, swerving around his stepmother's affections, as he made for the door, the road, the docks, the shore. A plank had already been lowered from the ship's deck by the time he arrived. Figures began to emerge onto land—one of which was the loveliest figure he'd ever seen with intelligent eyes that met his own.

But Ivan's stepmother would stand for no such interest, for she had recently become besotted by the young man herself. She instructed his tutor to stick him with a pin that would put him into an endless sleep so she herself could keep him forever. How the maiden tsar came to know of the scheme, Ivan never knew, but she revealed it in a note, recommended he kill his traitorous tutor, and confessed she was bound to set off again for the thrice tenth kingdom, where she reigned.

Did she invite him thither? You or I may question the existence of an actual invitation, but Ivan did not. He caught his tutor with the magic pin, beheaded the traitorous man, and set off to find the woman he would make his wife.

Quite the setup indeed, but that's how the story goes and thus how you shall hear it.

Ivan did not know how to find the thrice tenth kingdom, but he had heard tales of someone who did. He would not end up dead and shriveled without meeting the sea or sky, so he set off to find a baba yaga. His tutor would have scolded him for his belief in such old stories. His stepmother would have cooed and said how childish he could be, but realities don't care about others' beliefs. They simply are, and, he knew, the determined could find them.

"Fie, fie!" The shrieked words surprised him. Ivan had not realized how far into the forest he'd walked already. The wrinkled old woman stood outside the door of her chicken-legged hut, long arms crossed and embracing a massive stone pestle. "I smell the Russian scent, something I have not known for years." She blinked her beady eyes at Ivan. "Do you come of your own free will or by compulsion?"

"Good morning, baba yaga." Ivan bowed as he spoke, straightening as he considered how to answer. "I come largely by my own free will, mostly by compulsion. My own, no other's."

The old witch nodded and listened to his story of the maiden tsar but shook her head when he asked for the way to the thrice tenth kingdom.

"My younger sister likely knows. She may help you better than I."

The witch's hut turned around behind her, offering the old woman its front door.

Ivan thanked her, bowed again, and continued in the direction the baba yaga pointed. He trudged on for hours, out of one forest and into the next, where scurrying dark-furred animals leapt through the tangled branches overhead and sharp birdsong mimicked the shrill of screams.

When another strange hut appeared in an opening in the wood, Ivan was ready.

"Fie! Fie!" This younger baba yaga spat on the ground. "I smell the Russian scent, something I haven't known for years." Her eyes were just as beady, but she stood taller and more gracefully so. Shrews and moles nosed through the grass near her boney ankles. She rested her hand on the papery bark of a birch tree with twin trunks like a doorway she was ready to step through.

"Do you come of your own free will or by compulsion?"

"Good afternoon, baba yaga." Ivan again bowed as he spoke. "I come largely by my own free will, mostly by compulsion. My own, no other's."

The baba yaga nodded and listened to his story of the maiden tsar but shook her head when he asked for the way to the thrice tenth kingdom.

"My youngest sister will know the way," she answered, stripping a piece of bark from the tree with her long thin fingers then releasing it to flutter to the ground. "But beware, for she may try to eat you."

Ivan's full body tensed, but he thought of the maiden tsar in her far-off kingdom. He straightened his back and opened his mouth, but the baba yaga spoke first.

"Not all can escape her, but you have it in you." She peeled another strip of white papery bark, letting it drift down, down, down. "My youngest sister has three horns in her possession. Before you ask her anything about your maiden tsar, ask her if you can blow her horns."

Ivan, the merchant's son, nodded. The strips of birch slowly piled upon the ground.

"Blow softly on the first, harder on the next, and even harder on the third. This will protect you." And before Ivan could thank her or say anything else, the baba yaga walked between the tree trunks and disappeared.

He blew out a breath, pinched closed his eyes, and thought of that spider on the sill, dried and shriveled. But he wasn't that spider. Ivan pressed onward, out of this forest and into the next, and when the youngest baba yaga came into sight, Ivan was ready.

"Fie! Fie!" This youngest baba yaga sister shrieked the sound like a curse. "I smell the Russian scent, something I haven't known for years." Her eyes were almost hollow, her thin limbs appeared rooted to the ground. "Do you come of your own free will or by compulsion?"

"Good evening, baba yaga." Ivan bowed deeply as he spoke. "I come largely by my own free will, mostly by compulsion. My own, no other's. But may I blow your three horns?"

Her willowy hair blew in the breeze as she considered his question.

"One of my sisters told you to ask me this?" She didn't appear to require an answer but gestured to the three horns that sat nearby upon a fallen log.

Ivan stepped forward, blowing softly into the first, harder into the second, and harder still into the third. The baba yaga sprang at him, open mouthed and nails extended, but the skies filled with birds from every corner of the earth. Birds of prey and songbirds, storks and herons and gulls. The firebird itself swooped down to Ivan, and the merchant's son leapt upon its strong back. The baba yaga only managed to grab a handful of golden feathers as they lifted off to the sky through the haze of the clouds above, a momentary fog so dense it muddled his mind and his vision. But then they broke through on their way to the thrice tenth kingdom, where Ivan would seek the heart of the maiden tsar by meeting the sea and sky, holding strong to the faith held deep inside himself.

CHAPTER ELEVEN

On Faith, Paganism & Endurance

The quests of heroes are a common tale. Enter a protagonist one character trait away from perfection or with one happenstance restraining their potential. Ivan, the merchant's son, lived a confined life. Vasilisa's overbearing stepmother harassed her every movement. Prince Ivan's birthplace limited him as the third son. Yvashka could not control the strength of his body—and, I suppose, he had a bear's ear too.

In ancient Slavic allegories, gods and goddesses would help those in need overcome their obstacles and their flaws to become the better versions of themselves. Everyday people might wait for the judgment that only a goddess of the earth's balance could resolve. They would seek guidance from a presence so much greater than themselves, a quest not at its essence unfamiliar from contemporary spiritual journeys. Modern viewpoints assume that people thousands of years ago were far less advanced and civilized compared to people of today, but how much have we truly changed?

People try to deliberate and problem-solve. Our nature is to invent solutions. New year's resolutions seize upon this instinct and thus reenergize our intentions. Crossword puzzles and word games satisfy this same itch. Intricate, enigmatic tales enthrall us similarly as we try to unravel them alongside the characters. But not all challenges in life feel decipherable, and a goddess's interference, blessing, or punishment could give the solace and closure one might have craved.

Like heroes' quests, pilgrimages of enlightenment make for captivating stories. Under the veil of "folktale," Baba Yaga's ancient inheritance lingers. Terrified yet humbled, Vasilisa sought out Baba Yaga, as did Natasha and multiple Ivans. A meeting with the old boney-legged witch required bravery but also a recognition of the power of this woman in the woods, something unholy but simultaneously true.

For Baba Yaga, the heroes' and heroines' faith in her—against all odds and advice—captures the persistence of old beliefs amid a whirlwind of religious upheaval in the societies surrounding her. Time moves on, but her legacy remains, shrouded and mysterious in the darkest shadows of the woods. Many had forgotten her, and of those who remembered, most discounted her, avoided her, or doubted her significance. Her perception shriveled to a decrepit woman past her prime. Those few who recognized her importance did so stoically, covertly, and nonetheless with a lingering sense of dread.

Determination to keep an old faith and preserve ancient beliefs lingers within these protagonists' pilgrimages. The Telephone game twisted Baba Yaga's birthright with demonic declarations and witch hunts; however, she's remained the same force she has always been, a symbol of determination, balance, preparation, conscientious decision-making, and endurance from inside her fence of bones, where lights glow from the eyes of skulls on the fence posts.

When we have tales of plural baba yagas in the woods or sister baba yagas, like those in "Ivan & the Maiden Tsar," all the past goddesses who inspired her creation come to mind. They coexist in common memory, despite the fact that they originated in lands once cut off by mountains or seas. Thus, they are sisters. They are aunts. They are grandmother, mother, and child. Their differences are attributed to distinct baba yagas in nearby but dissimilar spaces. Barriers of time and geography disappear, and only whispers of what they once were remain. Archeologists have statuettes and icons. The rest of us have stories.

Clues are left for us like breadcrumbs dropped within the wood. Past sacrifices of the freshest foods endure in her particular nose. An affinity for certain mushrooms clings to classic illustrations and modern media like the fungi that they are. The highly civilized, female-reverent society of Trypillia fell. Later patriarchal societies tried to stamp out memory of the cultures and belief systems that came before. Mokosh's statue went up in Kiev in 980, and it tumbled down in 988, at the order of the same Prince Vladimir who had once commissioned it. Amid all the turmoil, little hints like Baba Yaga's strange solo in the court of Catherine the Great about hope and optimism for the future remind us of her complex legacy.

Examining how Baba Yaga's multifaceted role shifted to that of witch gives a greater context to her identity today, whether she is worshipped, studied, or reviled. Like Circe in *The Odyssey*, no better name existed for what she was, so the label of "witch" fell upon her for the world to remember. Of course, there the similarities end, for Baba Yaga is no enchantress. No, she is a natural force who holds the waters of life and death in her possession, whose flying mortar leads to magic possibilities, and whose horns call all the birds of all the lands for assistance. These tools of magic demonstrate her deep understanding of the world's secrets. And Baba Yaga's demonization and shift into "sorcery" is perhaps her most notable tale of all.

Stories of witches go back deep in time. One of the oldest known records is the story of King Saul seeking the witch of Endor, a story in the Book of Samuel dated roughly between 931 and 721 BCE. Yes, the Bible speaks of witches, if you didn't know. The Book of Exodus also holds the line, "thou shalt not suffer a witch to live," and later in Leviticus, witches are condemned to "be put to death . . . stone them with stones: their blood shall be upon them."

For the Christian church, the fight against those connected with "witchcraft" has a deep heritage. One of the earliest laws against paganism was put into effect under Theodosius I in the year 391. The Roman empire didn't stretch very far into Slavic lands at this point in time, but this was the beginning of a fight that would continue for centuries, if not thousands of years. Fascinatingly, Theodosius I may also be the Roman emperor who began the cancellation of the original Olympic games, with their Pagan practices at the core of his disdain. The gods and goddesses of Mount Olympus were once central to these games, after all. A certain historical irony exists for a witch born of Pagan goddesses farther north to appear in a cartoon created for the modern Olympic Games in 1980 in Moscow. Theodosius clearly lost that fight and then some.

Coming full circle, remember Baba Yaga's role in these cartoons wasn't purely as amusement but to act as an interfering nuisance, a metaphor for other countries interfering with Russia at the time. Politics and opinions of that recent historical moment aside, Theodosius I himself fit Baba Yaga's 1980 role quite aptly. What was he doing but interfering with everyone else? Yet faith in the old ways remained, no matter his rulings.

Nonetheless, Theodosius was only one leader out of many trying to snuff out long-standing belief and worship. Folktales themselves, with their remnants of old dogmas and rituals, preserving social values and cultural history, were banned in sections of Russia in the 1100s. These stories were considered obstacles to Christian conversation for rural populations who clung to old ways, but how do you ban a story spoken around a hearth fire? How do you forbid the words of a grandparent to a child? One answer became the weaving of familiar tales and rural knowledge into Christian allegories, as we've seen.

Needless to say, the term *pagan* had a different subtlety to its meaning when the word originated in the 1400s. Those who didn't try to understand the old faiths wanted a common name for the people who believed in them—specifically beliefs outside of Christianity, Judaism, and Islam. These many faiths, with their varied deities and rituals, stretched across lands but frequently drifted away from major cities, where newer ideas took hold. Thus, the etymological roots of *pagan* come from a Latin root meaning "country dweller." Interestingly, the word *heathen* has a similar root, originally meaning a "heath dweller." Massive cultural centers experienced waves of new ideas, but for many farther off, old beliefs, traditions, and ways of life remained.

In early reflections of these contrasts, the word *pagan* was also understood by the people of this time to mean "civilian," in contrast with a "soldier of Christ," a common title claimed by early Christians. A civilian versus a soldier. A battle had begun from these earliest days, if only linguistically at first, with few hints of what words like *pagan* and *heathen* would become. The social transformation of these ideas was not instantaneous.

We have previously discussed the "Worthies" woven into medieval tapestries, the men and women of disparate faiths living up to medieval chivalric ideals. These were Christian, Jewish, and Pagan individuals. Clearly, if *pagan* had a connection with the demonic at this time in history, different language would have been used. The expansion of the Christian church was becoming its own quest. Snuffing out these country religions became a goal of newly coronated princes, kings, and emperors. Baba Yaga's identity began its jarring rearrangement during this time period, but no matter if lingering as a goddess, a balancing force, or a wise old herbalist, faith in her presence remained.

Meanwhile, elsewhere in Europe, a long-brewing revolution picked up force. The Bible spoke of witches and how to punish such a woman, but a new manuscript rejuvenated these old ideas with brutal ferocity. The 1486 book, *Malleus Maleficarum*, or "The Witch's Hammer," sold more copies than any other book, only excluding the Bible, for more than one hundred years. Written by Johann Sprenger, dean of the University of Cologne, and Heinrich Kraemer, professor of theology at the University of Salzburg and inquisitor in the Tirol region of Austria, *Malleus Maleficarum* examined folktales and superstitions as much as any other source, quickly becoming the standard guidebook for identifying witch-craft and exterminating witches.

A connection between old magic and the devil, who was once con-sidered a minor character in the Bible, is also rooted in this point in time. The devil grew as an adversary to all that was good and holy, and those who believed in or practiced witchcraft were named as his followers.

Female goddesses and the matriarchal nature of numerous pre-Christian civilizations were lost when their artifacts were buried at best and destroyed at worst. Nevertheless, Baba Yaga is known for her wiles. Amid witch hunts and new religious pressures, Baba Yaga seems to have picked up her own shattered remains, reforming into an alarming new likeness, taking up the mantle of "witch" if that was all the world would remember of her. And her stories whispered on.

The invention of the printing press could have been a bastion for the preservation of culture and history, but like so much else during this time, printed words emerged with extreme religious focus, especially in Eastern Europe. While the first printing in Cyrillic was in 1491 by German-born Schweipolt Fiol, who published "Oktoikh" through Fiol Press in Kraków, Poland, printing presses were slow to expand in Slavic regions. Ivan Fyodorov, known as one of the fathers of Eastern Slavonic printing, led the first confirmed publication signed by a Russian publisher in 1553, and Ukraine's first known printing presses began in approxi-mately 1580, including one founded at Ostroh in Volhynia by Prince Konstantyn Ostrozky. Many monks and religious institutions led these presses, including the Kievan Brotherhood, and a short time after they emerged, extreme restrictions bound them. Religious texts were the most common publications. Folktales and legacies of any lingering Slavic dei-ties were not materials of interest or acceptability.

Not only stories but language itself was under pressure. Peter I of Russia banned all printing in the Ukrainian language in 1720. He com-manded only Russian to be published. Loss of language, as we know, leads to loss of cultural identity and the forfeiture of familiar stories and turns of phrase specific to a place and time. By the time written Ukrainian reemerged and was newly standardized in the 1800s, generations had gone by. Literature in older Ukrainian became more difficult to decipher, less accessible to the those reclaiming their cultural inheritance. How a character like Baba Yaga sustained in oral storytelling, sometimes hiding herself in lyrics of familiar songs, is a testament to not only humanity's love of a good tale but to the weight of her presence in Slavic culture. She hunkered down as best she could while simultaneously stealing away to other lands, as only a folktale witch was able. Thus, her tales continued on with countless variations, and faith in her remained. Religious practices no longer maintained the goddess in the woods, but she held fast in the spoken word.

As we've seen, Baba Yaga was well known and fairly well defined by the time of her first appearance in print in *The Russian Grammar* in 1755. Her acknowledgment in a Russian text is almost revolutionary in this moment, but here she is in a study of world cultures, beliefs, and language itself. I almost want to applaud her endurance. May we all have such stamina.

The fact that my own grandmother believed in the existence of Baba Yaga, a horrifying witch deep within the woods, speaks to this character's lingering legacy. She wasn't merely a story. She was more than a morality tale. She was a legacy of thousands of years of persistence, determination, and identity that refused erasure.

In her tales, the heroes and heroines who seek her believe that with her help they can do the impossible. Prince Ivan on his firebird hunt. Ivan the merchant's son seeking the thrice tenth kingdom. Let the number of Ivans in these tales not distract us. Finding Baba Yaga is an act of faith. She is forbidden yet essential to everything. She is dangerous yet transformative in the plot of heroes' lives. She is a guide who counsels, educates, and further prepares these protagonists, who would be unable to complete their quests without her. Their tenacious ongoing belief in her power is both unlikely and astounding.

Youthful protagonists are willing to explore the mysterious and unknown. Call them brash, bold, or naïve, but their interest and pursuit of the "pagan" leads to heroes' journeys the world remembers. Many adult characters might not accept belief in old magic, or they have reputations to uphold—reputations built upon new systems that looked down upon ancient spiritualism. Ivan's tutor, for example, if not beheaded, would have scoffed at his quest for the baba yagas' aid. But these young characters keep faith in Baba Yaga and all she represents, especially when no one else in their world dares to believe or remember.

Stories linger, and stories endure. After the eventual reemergence and surge of folktales' popularity in Eastern Europe, certain government institutions took it upon themselves to edit the stories' content and subtexts—ensuring ideas they approved of were well-defined. Specific tropes began to arise. Modest, working-class heroes overcame greedy, rich villains with the help of a generous and trustworthy leader. Evil witches would eat you if you stepped out of line beyond desired ideals and behaviors. Censorship and editorial boards were no longer tied to religion but to government propaganda campaigns.

In 1928, the Russian Association of Proletarian Writers formed to take the place of multiple earlier creative organizations. Under their guidance, literature and storytelling became a tool to further communist ideals, and art for the sake of exploration, reflection, creative curiosity, or pure entertainment was shunned at best, condemned or destroyed at worst. Forced silences fell over writers who had once been considered literary masters. State officials skilled in propaganda but otherwise little experienced in the craft of the written word took the reins of literary journals and other publishers.

The five-year period when the Russian Association of Proletarian Writers was at its height was the same time frame as the murders of the

Ukrainian kobzars. Both efforts had the unwavering blessing of Stalin, leaving us one of the greatest reminders that applied then and applies now: stories can indeed impact the populace. To yoke the stories and the storytellers is to restrain free thought and free societies. Once again, old conversations are as applicable as ever.

The world tells us so much. Determining what to believe is a challenge that only intensifies with time and technology, but there's something to be said for believing in characters that refuse to quit—in an old witch's persistence as well as your own. You too can pick up the shattered pieces of all you've ever been, reconfiguring them as you'd like then continuing onward with dogged persistence, having faith in yourself even when the world doesn't appear to be on your side.

Forbid her stories, demonize her, or reframe her as a morality tale, but after all the witch hunts and rewrites, Baba Yaga remains. Some still call her worship-worthy, seeking her out as heroes and heroines have of old. For aren't we all one flaw away from perfection? One happenstance restraining our potential? May we all be such forces audiences need to reconsider.

12

"NONY & THE BOY OF STICKS"

ot so long ago and not so far away, a wife aching for a child could rock and bounce a bundle of sticks into life and name the babe Peter. In the house next door, an anonymous girl felt scant and worthless compared to such enchantments, she who was merely made of flesh and nonmagical bones.

The anonymous girl is never the protagonist of this story, but let's weave the tale like we're rebraiding its heroine's hair. Anonymous no more, let's call her Nony.

Nony wove silver threads into the strongest of fishing lines the day her neighbor sang lullabies to her bundle of sticks swaddled in scarves. The lonely wife tickled its middle and cooed in that way all mothers know, until the bundle cooed back. A birth is always miraculous, so what's one more kind of miracle? Nony was young, but she'd already seen all kinds.

Peter's body grew. His curiosity did too. Nony wove more fishing line, for the little boy this time, before she kneaded her bread, folded her laundry, and swept the steps that always became dusty once again.

However, Nony always left her to-do list behind when Peter set out in his little boat. She persuaded the sturgeon in the water to tug the beautiful silver fishing line farther from the shore whenever she saw the boney-legged stride of Baba Yaga. For Baba Yaga came often. Watching. Waiting. Planning Peter's capture so she could prod his magical soul. Baba Yaga loved children, especially magical ones, but as all children have a touch of magic within, maybe the boy once made of sticks was no different from any other.

Far off on the lake, the boy baited a hook. The sturgeon swam underneath. Nony's strong silver fishing line dipped into the water, a scratch upon the reflection of the overhead clouds. On the shore, Baba Yaga scratched a stick in the sand. She had a plan for what her own best bait would be. She twisted and crumpled her voice to sound like the boy's mother then called out his name.

Peter looked up from his fishing. The old witch called out again, smiling with her sharp iron teeth while ducking into the shadows of the water reeds and the woolly-fruit sedge. Nony tucked herself behind a willow as the boy stood in his boat, balancing on the unsteady water, before sitting back down. She begged the sturgeons to pull him farther.

But Baba Yaga wanted the boy once made of sticks even more than the lonely wife once wanted a child. So the old witch jumped in her flying mortar, steered her way with a pestle, and soared into town. Arriving at the blacksmith's door, she ordered him to make her a new voice out of fire and iron and sparks, and with fear in his eyes, he did as she asked.

With her new voice in her mouth, Baba Yaga returned to the lake. This time when she called, the boy immediately smiled. Sometimes, he still had sticks for brains. The sturgeon whipped underneath him, but without the silver line, they could do nothing. When he reached the shore, Baba Yaga snatched him up, leaving his boat, his pole, the silver line, and the sturgeon behind.

And if you might say that poor Nony remains distant from her own story, this is where her tale takes a turn, for protagonists we all might be, but so much depends on what chapter of our life we're living.

Nony, who had been underestimated all her life, knew how to run, how to pump her arms and lift her legs and dash like something wild and untamed, like something that could follow a witch's trail into the wood. She rarely dared to let her hair loose, to let her cheeks redden and sweat dampen her brow. The dark forest had been her only haven for such compulsions. The old witch didn't know how fast Nony herself could fly.

She tracked the path of severed branches and splintered mountain pines. The magic broom that flew behind Baba Yaga hadn't brushed all of her trail away.

Deeper and deeper into the forest, Nony shadowed the most shadowy of all, until she almost tripped over a small cat who stretched out to nuzzle her leg. Nony reached into her pocket and gave the cat a piece of braided bread she'd saved for Peter. The cat purred and trotted up a chicken-scratch of a path Nony had almost run by, a path leading to a tiny hut, with a peaked roof, inside a fence of bones.

Nony's pulse hammered in her rib cage. She tried to steady her breath as she reached down to stroke the cat who had returned to sit down beside her, licking up the last of the breadcrumbs.

"Are you seeking work or shunning it?"

The voice made Nony spin around. Behind her stood Baba Yaga, iron teeth parted as she smiled.

"Seeking it," Nony answered quickly, dropping into a quick curtsy, hoping to hide the sweat on her brow.

"Good," said the witch. "Then make me my supper. Tomorrow, I'll give you pine pitch to fix my roof."

Nony nodded and, forcing herself to breathe calmly, darted inside, where many fine meats filled the shelves. She washed her hands, felt the old witch watching, then pulled out ingredients for bread, finding familiarity as she soon plunged her fingers into the quickly made dough. As she sprinkled her palms and fingers with more flour, something swayed in the window. A child-sized cage hung just outside.

Peter's fingers looked as thin as the sticks they had once been as they poked through the bars. Onions had been sliced and spread about him. Frilly sprigs of dill sprinkled about his hair and down his collar. Nony looked away when the witch came near. She pressed the heels of her hands into her dough. The cat wove around her ankles. The fine meats were seasoned. And when the feast was ready, Baba Yaga ate it all, licking her lips, tossing only the tiniest of bones to the little cat when she was done.

"When Baba Yaga sleeps," the cat whispered in a purr Nony could somehow understand, "you can escape with the boy once made of sticks."

Nony stroked the cat, who released a more usual purr, then the girl's attention snagged on the bucket of black pine pitch sitting ready for her work in the morning. She closed her eyes, nodded to herself, then waited for night, for the moon to be covered in clouds and the stars to pause sleepily as they twinkled.

When all was so, Nony lifted the bucket in her arms and tiptoed to the bed in the corner of the hut. She rubbed the black sticky pitch over the sleeping Baba Yaga's eyes, carefully watching the old witch's breath as it rose and fell, rose and fell.

The door of Peter's cage rattled as Nony opened it, and she winced. Behind them, Baba Yaga stirred in the darkness. When the boy's muffled grunts caught the old witch's ears as he squeezed from the cage, Baba Yaga tilted her head and sat up. She tried to open her eyes, but they were sealed shut.

"Cat!" she screeched. "Use your claws to slice what covers my eyes!"

"No," said the cat, weaving around the legs of the bed. "For you have never given me more than bones and complaints. The girl gave me food and kindness."

Baba Yaga screeched, and far off already, Nony caterwauled a reply that echoed out across the dark pine forest behind her.

"Anonymous girls don't deserve your attention," the old witch hissed.

But, naturally, they always do. For they can climb out of someone else's story, brush off the stray onions and dill, and claim it as their own. You just never know when it will happen.

CHAPTER TWELVE

Baba Yaga, Darkness & the Shadow Self

A shadow on the edge of the lake, watching, waiting as a young boy all alone sails in his small boat. A creature with holes for eyes and hands like claws, who travels through the skies. The guide of souls to the world beyond the living. The destroyer of that which is out of balance. These somber and startling facets of Baba Yaga's existence aren't all falsifications made by church slander and witch-hunters. Baba Yaga's darkness is undeniably a major part of who she is. She has been a partner with Death. She lives in the bleakest, unknown realm of the forest. She has been the judge of actions and the punisher of the unworthy. When imagined as a plow, tearing apart the earth for something new to grow, we cannot ignore how violently the dirt crumbles and how rocks scatter at her whim. To not understand her darkness is to not understand the woman herself.

In Nony's story, commonly titled "Baba Yaga and the Servant Girl," we see Baba Yaga in one of her three classic forms. Here we do not have Baba Yaga the mentor, nor Baba Yaga the donor. We see Baba Yaga as the pure villain, the witch who steals the child for no reason other than her own wicked nature, her own selfish desire for something magical yet somehow unknown to her. The tale of "Baba Yaga's Black Geese" weaves her in a similar fashion.

In a 1932 Russian cartoon version of this story, the protagonist is only Peter, and he's a human boy, nothing magic made of sticks. He isn't fooled by Baba Yaga calling from the shore, pretending to be his mother, until the blacksmith makes a new voice for the witch, as the story goes. However, in this rendition, there's no anonymous servant girl. Instead, he escapes his eventual capture by scrambling up a tree. The crafty old witch then returns to the blacksmith, and he gives her new iron teeth to gnaw down Peter's perch. Iron teeth? Familiar indeed. Slapstick comedy ensues—and I say this literally. Many sticks and branches slap the old witch as the hunt continues. Finally, a collection of white geese saves Peter, and, in short, seeing centuries-old tales in grayscale, early animation allows for a new perspective. Misha the Bear's animated fights against Baba Yaga in cartoons a half century later, around the 1980 Olympics, have a similarly fascinating but jarring effect. We cannot turn away from the villain, while our hearts may cheer for the hero's victory.

Baba Yaga's multiplicities add to her legacy in the modern world, but her wickedness is the role she most epitomizes in contemporary media. Her malevolence has something more to say. Baba Yaga is a familiar threat, connected with others we recognize well. She is the anxiety that brings out the best and worst of us. She is the gift of the darkness and the necessity of its existence for balance in our lives. She is our permission to rage and to acknowledge our own darker impulses, giving us accessible means to process the disorder lingering all around us.

Familiar folktales can be introductions to the unsettling realities that can exist in life. Little Red Riding Hood's big bad wolf slinks onto the path beside her. Jack's giant in the sky appears right when all is going so well. When invited to walk in a protagonist's shoes by reading or listening along with them, we face their challenges at a safe distance. The big bad wolf will not swallow us up after poor old sick Granny. The giant will not crush us at the top of the beanstalk where we know we shouldn't be. In spite of this, stress, quick decision-making, courage, and persistence are top of mind. We know the underdog, because when absorbed in a story, we are the underdog. Or we are the bold hero, confronting the distressing against all odds, riding atop the firebird, magic horn to our lips. Chaos repeatedly crashes onto the scene, disrupting both routine moments and our greatest quests. We don't have to be named Jack or Ivan to sympathize.

As storytelling creatures, people are held rapt by a good tale. Metaphors are more than human invention. They are instincts and gut punches captured in ink and time, experiments with naming that which is beyond words yet still on the tip of our tongues. Shifting everyday reality into the grandiose and the exaggerated allows our lives too to transform, for we are built to be lost in a story.

We want to be the protagonist of our own lives, so we reframe our own memories and pursuits accordingly. It has always been so. In this way, unknown illnesses originate in demonic possession. Perfect mothers die, and monstrous stepmothers take their place when adolescent worlds shift, tug, and recalibrate relationships. Professional nuisances become personal nemeses. Sports team rivalries become battles of good versus evil. Gaining a desperate desire by making a choice that goes against our moral code is doing a deal with the devil, and we already know whatever follows will not end well. Difficulties arise out of nowhere, behemoths that have the ability to crush villages, swallow passersby, and otherwise destroy fully content lives.

Baba Yaga exists amid such traditions. She is the foreboding always lurking beyond what we can see. She is the threat in the darkness, or the trick we know not to fall for but are drawn to all the same. World folklore fosters connections far beyond matters of snakes and hedgehogs.

The "AT index system," originally named for Finnish folklorist Antti Aarne and American folklorist Stith Thompson, attempts to bring uniformity of discussion between such stories. Plot concepts echo across oral tales told by disparate regions and their tellers. Similar tales repeatedly arise. This original system, created by Aarne in 1910, built off of earlier categorization systems and was updated by Thompson in 1928 and then again in 1961. As of 2004, the system expanded again and is now commonly discussed as the "ATU index," after contributions by German folklorist Hans-Jörg Uther. What was once an analysis of European folktale types is slowly expanding.

Some of Baba Yaga's most famous stories parallel others in the world, but her tales have shaped still others in similar ways. Some stories travel the globe, or perhaps they simply exist in the zeitgeist of humanity. This familiarity allows for deeper understanding of the dark tales people have always told as warnings to keep each other safe and as reminders not to become too complacent in the comfort of their lives.

So into the woods we go to seek Baba Yaga, whether her stories fit tale types or not. And in these woods, where the black geese and crows are her companions, we may find our solace or our demise. It depends on the witch you discover, not necessarily Baba Yaga versus Ježibaba versus Baba Croanta—but rather, which version of the story makes all the difference.

One aspect I appreciate about many Slavic tales is the acknowledgment that when good conquers evil, that's not the end of the story. Remember, Baba Yaga may die a fiery death in a raging river of flame. She may be appeased with tasks completed, staying behind while the protagonist goes free. However, as both the storyteller and the listener know, the old witch is never gone for good.

She will return in another tale, another circumstance, reminding the reader to remain vigilant. If you're not prepared for the darkness, it might make you fall apart. This is a lesson from folktales but also a lesson my grandparents carried away from their war-torn experiences of World War II. Having known the darkest of humanity and the struggle for life itself, they lived fully appreciating the love of family and the possibilities of a future lost to so many. They told stories of war to pass on the scariest realities they knew, preparing younger generations for the truth that life can change in an instant. They ensured we understood that while we could not always control the events around us, we could control our preparation for and our reaction to those events. Baba Yaga tales serve the same purpose, albeit with the absurdity of her chicken-legged hut by her side.

As heroes and psychologists know, benefits arise from confronting our fears.

Anxiety is our body's way of preparing us for the worst, our imagination's strategy session to enable us to confront our reality, whatever it may be. That reality is usually not as bad as we envision, but being ready for old witches in the woods can be the groundwork for a stronger sense of self. Furthermore, acknowledging that our fears are the result of something disquieting around us and that something needs to change is empowering. When we reframe our fear as a call to action, we can examine what steps we can take to better the circumstance. Nony discovered this reality. We all can. If people didn't acknowledge their apprehensions, humans would have died off long ago. When we are struck down by a witch or our own inner voices, recognizing the strength behind our instincts can be a transformative coping mechanism.

Fear can also inspire changed behavior in ourselves. We can know something, sure, but until faced with mortal peril, we may not encounter the true motivation to act differently. A survivor of a near-death experience may well reform their everyday bad habits that brought them to such a brink. Near misses have lessons if we dare to listen. Similarly, Yvashka with the Bear's Ear knew Baba Yaga would try to take her bite. His friends had clearly suffered. Fear grew. Fear lingered. A motivated protagonist invents new ways of living and a trap or two to ensure his survival.

Moreover, exploring the darker impulses of Baba Yaga's stories also acknowledges that the darkness is not always prompted by external circumstances like witches flying overhead in the night. Baba Yaga tales speak to our own shadow selves too, whether we want to admit such pieces of ourselves or not. We connect with the fearful old woman with her magic ways in the woods when Prince Ivan and his wolf knock on Baba Yaga's door. We have our days when we understand the motivations behind her black geese and her frustrations when her glorious plan of a

golden ring backfires in her face. We would never—no, never—act as she does. But pretending that we could can be satisfying.

When Swiss psychiatrist and psychoanalyst Carl Jung said, "One does not become enlightened by imagining figures of light, but by making the darkness conscious," he could have been speaking of Baba Yaga herself. Jung's theories of "the shadow self," the darker impulses that exist within all of us, are at the essence of who this old Slavic witch frequently shows herself to be.

As much as we want to imagine ourselves above our baser natures, animalistic tendencies linger. We may not have bears' ears or wolves as helpmates, but fear taps into deeper instincts. We strive to be moral beings driven by our best intentions, like Vasilisa or Ivan, prince or otherwise, on his better days. But we aren't always. We have our imperfections and moments when our worst selves shine through, when our teeth grind and we want to strike out—if only within the safety of our imaginations.

Frustrations impact our internal and external reactions. Our desires aren't always in line with societal standards. Actions of rudeness, arrogance, aggression, and defensiveness can be reframed as self-preservation. But that's just our shadow self talking. That's Baba Yaga and her bold embrace of the darkness that balances the light.

Confident in her years and with full control of both her positive and negative attributes, she has no shame and no fear of disapproval. Her shadow isn't something she hides. Call it what you will—your evil twin, your lower self, your dark side—baser tendencies exist within us all. Sometimes we dream them. Sometimes we repress them. Yet learning how to acknowledge them can be freeing, not released in a tirade but calling that tiny whisper of an impulse "Baba Yaga," giving her a little nod, and moving on with your day. Acting upon that temper that arises may not be advisable, but to be human is to have imperfections. We don't need to hide from our internal notions. These urges can be outlets for pieces of ourselves we rarely explore, and allowing for their existence gives us greater possibilities, as Nony herself discovers.

Black sticky pine pitch can fix a roof or blind a witch. Nony's baser creativity in this case allows her to survive.

Casual stargazers and scientists alike understand nature's need for the darkness as well as the daytime. Light pollution destroys more than views of the Milky Way. Insects are thrown by false light. Bats need the dark to survive their nocturnal lifestyle. People need to balance their light and their darkness too. A good villain makes us reexamine who we are, who we've been, and who we could be. She gives us a reprieve from the constant flashes of brilliance in heroes and heroines that demand our attention. For who could live up to such ideals?

The scales of storytelling are balanced by characters like Baba Yaga the true witch, giving us permission to rage, even if we would never follow her lead beyond our own imaginations. She gives us permission to scream into the void, cackle at the darkness, and vent our anxieties at the wind, even if nothing more than a passing gaggle of geese is listening.

We might work out our fears and frustrations with a hard run, a workout, a meditation, or quality time with family or friends. But not Baba Yaga. She's a solo soul if there ever was one. And rage against the world? That might just be her specialty.

We can hide from the shadows or accept the gifts hidden within them. Nony's persistence amid her anxieties, one step forward then another into the woods, walking then sprinting at full speed, seeking to discover the root of the panic inside, is worth further consideration. She recognizes the darkness in the world, and facing it enables the start of her own story. She accesses her own visceral, undisciplined creativity to survive and save Peter too. She, like countless other heroines, reminds us that a sense of foreboding can break us or embolden us. The path is yours to choose, and Baba Yaga gives us a greater perspective on choosing well.

13

"MARIA MOREVNA"

ou might be familiar with leaders in halls of thought, who are rarely the same as the fiercest combatants on the battle-field; nor do these two qualities frequently merge with the disciplined actions necessary to truly care for a nation's people. Yet Queen Maria Morevna was known throughout her kingdom for all these aptitudes. And yes, she was a woman. Does it need to be said?

When she took a husband, Ivan, who was a prince and who became her partner and king, she only made one request of him to ensure the best for her kingdom: not to ever open the door of the locked closet in the dungeon.

Simple requests can be the hardest to follow. She knew this, but she had faith in the discipline of her new bridegroom. She had chosen him for many reasons, he who knew falcon and eagle and raven as kin. Thus, Maria Morevna didn't give the guidance a second thought as she rode off to her next battle under the waxing crescent moon, leaving Ivan behind.

But Ivan had always been a curious man. He pressed his ear to the forbidden wooden door deep within the dungeon of the castle. Groans of agony splintered the silence within. Eyebrows raised, the once-prince-now-king paced the corridor. Back and forth, and back and forth. His steps shuffled against the stone floor. The groans became louder. Sweat trickled into one eye, and he wiped it away, halting his footsteps directly in front of the closet.

A groan came again, earsplitting, or maybe fracturing his very mind. Ivan put his hand to the doorknob. A pitiful plea for help met his ears, and the once-prince-now-king couldn't help it. He swung the closet open.

In the shadowed interior, chains contained neither man nor beast, but the great wizard Koscheii the Deathless. While countless had tried, Maria Morevna had been the only warrior to ever trap and contain him. She hadn't even bragged that it had been so. Admiration for his wife flickered across Ivan's heart for just a moment before Koscheii's form disappeared into a whirlwind, first propelling Ivan back out of the doorway then gusting out of sight.

Ivan didn't know how, but he heard Maria Morevna's far-off scream. He pressed his forehead to the cold stone walls of the dungeon. He knew he couldn't beat Koscheii by strength, wit, or bravery. But there was one who had horses faster than the old wizard. Ivan needed to find Baba Yaga, beyond the thrice nine lands in the thirtieth kingdom, across the fiery river and deep in the woods beyond. She was the only one who could conquer the great deathless wizard. In truth, Baba Yaga was the only being Koscheii truly feared.

Setting off as quickly as he could, Ivan didn't think to include food among his provisions for his journey. He set his route, rode as far as his old horse would take him, then left him at a favorite watering hole and continued on by foot. Step by step. Through fields and hills. Past cliffs and bogs and caves. Exhausted and hungry by the time he journeyed through thrice seven lands, Ivan ducked when a woodpecker swooped before him to land upon a tree a mere stone's throw away. Ivan picked up a pebble, imagining a bird dinner.

"Drop the rock," said a little voice from a branch by his side. A second redheaded woodpecker gazed into Ivan's eyes, and Ivan knew not what to do but gaze back. "Drop the rock and keep blood from our feathers, and we will watch out for you the same."

Ivan let the rock tumble from his grip, not answering the bird, but putting up his bare hand to show he understood. The pine needles under his feet silenced his footsteps as he forced himself onward, but not long after, he paused when he heard buzzing. Cocking his head to the side, Ivan closed his eyes until his ears led him to a hive full of honey.

"Stop!" cried the queen bee. "Let us be, and I promise we will return the favor someday."

Ivan's stomach grumbled, but he nodded and continued on. The dark forest grew darker. Bracken and snakeweed tugged at his ankles.

Blackthorn blocked his path, turning him in another direction, then another. A rustle under a barren dwarf cherry tree made him jerk around.

A lion cub chased its tail, and all Ivan could see was the possibility of a feline supper. King of beasts for king of man.

"Don't you dare," growled a lioness, crouched in more blackthorn on his opposite side. "You have your dagger and your sword, but we have done nothing to you. Let us be, and we will return the favor."

Ivan's head ached. His limbs felt heavy. The bare cherry tree seemed to mock him. But he nodded and continued on, chewing upon tree bark to satiate the hunger overtaking him. When the river of fire came to his sight and its crackling came to his ears, Ivan fell to his knees, desperation intermingled with exhaustion. He wiped his sweaty brow with a handkerchief he'd taken from Maria Morevna's nightstand. He was so weak, but rage found its way, pricking at his throat like the thorns he'd pushed through, throbbing on his skin like the venomous bite of something that had slithered away unseen.

Hollering at the setting sun, Ivan shook his fists and cursed Koscheii's name, the handkerchief in his hand warming to a glow as he did so. Shocked, he dropped it, but as the fabric fluttered to the ground, a great bridge appeared high over the licking flames of the river.

Maria Morevna's handkerchief. Had she known this magic? But Ivan knew that of course she did, because his new wife was more astounding than beasts or breath or birds. He stepped off the bridge on the other side, his feet sure of where they were going—into the darkness, never to veer astray.

Boney-legged Baba Yaga stood in front of her chicken-legged hut when he finally found it.

"Dearest grandmother," Ivan rasped, collapsing upon the forest floor. "Your fastest steed. Please . . ."

"Have you come on your own accord or by some other's compulsion?"

"I thought to come to you," the once-prince-now-king answered, lips barely off the ground. "For no one else could save Maria Morevna or strike terror into someone they call Deathless."

The old witch hobbled toward him on her skinny legs, studying his face and perhaps his soul, though no, her eyes were unseeing, turbulent clouds of gray and white. "Let me feed you, for you'll need your strength." She pinched his face in her hands, turning it from side to side on the ground where he lay. The light of the full moon shone down upon them. Ivan didn't know how many days had passed since he'd last seen his wife.

"I could keep you forever, but I will only do so for three days. If none of my horses escape before that time, you may have the fastest one."

Thus, a challenge was set forth. And thus, Baba Yaga ordered her horses to stray. But day one, they were chased back by the squawks and beating wings of thousands of birds; day two, they were herded by bees; day three, they were corralled by lions. Ivan crossed his arms before his chest as he met Baba Yaga's cloudy gaze after the final day. She crossed her own arms, pointing her long nose toward the stables where all her horses were safely tucked away.

"Don't do things like this to your wife." She scowled. "Powerful women can indeed be stronger with a partner, but she might look toward me and realize it's not always so."

Once-prince-now-king Ivan nodded and spoke his thanks to her before taking the gift of her fastest horse and tearing off to Koscheii's kingdom. When he freed Maria Morevna, she only shook her head at him and grabbed the reins from his hands.

The waning moon shone overhead. Far away, the old witch Baba Yaga cackled. They didn't know how they heard. Then grasping the great steed Ivan had acquired, Maria Morevna tried to regain her faith in her bridegroom. She had chosen him for many reasons, he who knew falcon and eagle and raven as kin, he who met Baba Yaga and won her fastest horse. Whether they'd be caught and killed by Koscheii the Deathless or whether she'd be able to bind his magic once again remained to be seen. But facing the impossible and finding a way are the path of the philosopher, the warrior, and the disciplined—and, certainly, the path of queens who are all these. Does it even need to be said?

CHAPTER THIRTEEN

Feminist, Mother, Crone

"Maria Morevna" is one of my favorite Baba Yaga stories, not only for Baba Yaga's part of the tale but also for the heroine's. Although much of Maria Morevna's time is spent locked in the dungeon of an evil wizard, her existence is central to the story as are the many ways women can demonstrate power. While the old trope of the damsel in distress is present, so many others are shattered. No naïve whim or poorly disguised trick trapped her there. No, Maria Morevna is a force—strategic, brilliant, and formidable in countless ways. Her downfall stemmed from a foolish prince turned king, and the happily-ever-after marriage plot too is turned on its head. Then who is the savior who can defeat the immortal wizard, Koscheii the Deathless? Certainly not Maria Morevna's Prince Charming. Instead, an old woman hidden in the woods is the only one who can enable her freedom. Baba Yaga is never easy to work with, but she has the answers to everything.

Baba Yaga stories have many teachings behind the tales, but this one specifically speaks to the reality of what a woman can be and what a woman can do—not only if she's a beautiful young princess and not only if she finds a husband, but who she can be on her own. Her age and appearance are inconsequential to the tale. From traditional juggles of homelife excellence to stunning shows of intelligence, diligence, and strength in traditionally male spheres, Baba Yaga's greatest enduring contribution to world storytelling is arguably how she recasts the roles of women's lives through her own blind-eyed lens.

The shifts of the moon itself echo a global storytelling leitmotif, calling to mind the manifold powers of women and their ties to the lunar cycle. The new moon, the waxing moon, the full moon, the waning moon. From nothing to growing maiden, to rounded mother, then shrinking crone—for what more is a woman than these, as world stories have said? But delivering the unexpected is Baba Yaga's specialty. She is known as a great midwife after all.

Maria Morevna is not technically a maiden, but she plays the strong, young woman's role in this story. The audience of her tale quickly knows her strength is so much greater than any weapon in her hand or the physical muscle behind it. The medieval tapestries that captured the "Worthies" had a similar presentation of female distinction. Many of the women who exemplified the best of womanhood upon these artworks were well versed in battle, yet these women were not dressing up to be a different shape of a man. Nor was Maria Morevna adding shoulder pads to her straight-waisted power suits or her chain mail armor.

Within this story, we see the strength of a young woman at marrying age; we see the strength of a mother-like figure looking over a lost youth in need—for isn't this precisely Ivan's position?—and finally we see the strength of an old wisewoman with many answers and some good advice. Maiden, mother, crone. These unique identities are also known as the triple goddesses, each with their role in the divine feminine. They have been skillfully woven, not within renowned threads this time but amid world folktales that linger over centuries and beyond, shaping the world and our perceptions as much as any other narrative that fills our ears.

"Maiden, mother, crone" may be the familiar refrain, but in our discussion, let's rename the role of the "maiden" as "feminist," for virginity and marital status aren't necessary pieces of the conversation. Energized and increasingly aware, learning self-sufficiency and ready to take on the world, a newly born feminist need not be young. She must only be an egalitarianist on the brink of her newfound capabilities. No incendiary politics need apply.

Baba Yaga waits for such girls and occasionally seeks them out, does she not? If they are disappointing, she will threaten to eat them, but any capable, confident young woman who responds to her with respectfulness, thoughtfulness, a good heart, and all the bravery she can find within herself is welcomed into the old witch's house. The heroines endure trials, and in this way, each girl's rite of passage allows her to seize upon renewed readiness to find her way in the world. Conventions of a traditional wife—such as cooking, cleaning, and waiting upon another—are a part of this, as we've seen. Again, we must acknowledge the place and time of the creation of any story. But these budding feminists are not merely preparing for married life. They are preparing themselves to step into their greater potentials, recognizing the profound strength within, the selflessness that may be required of them in motherhood, and the dignity and insight held within the age-spotted grasp of an older woman, something they may have once initially feared.

In many versions of Vasilisa's tale, after she leaves Baba Yaga's house with her fire-filled skull in her hands, after her stepmother and stepsisters are turned to dust, our heroine goes off to a nearby village. There, she befriends an old woman, who not only takes her in but also teaches her how to weave. This mutually beneficial partnership between the young and the old empowers them both, and in a short time, Vasilisa becomes the most renowned weaver in her village. Did she design medieval tapestries with remarkable women upon them? Who knows? Did her magnificent work catch the eye of the son of the tsar? Indeed. But skipping over the familiar marriage plot for a moment, let's return to the partnership of young and old, the strength of women at different ages, and the recognition of stronger possibilities when women come together. Feminism hides within Vasilisa, Maria Morevna, Nony, and so many more.

The old woman of the woods might not have gone to suffragette rallies or bared her breasts in more recent "sextremist" protests. She wouldn't don a white dress or a sash to raise her voice with her sisters. Yet, as we know, feminism appears in many forms and has many definitions. It also appears in Eastern European history books and texts of classic mythology if we know where to look.

We've discussed the society of Trypillia, a civilization stretching across present-day Ukraine, Moldova, and Romania that held a special reverence toward the sacred feminine roughly 7,000 years ago; however, another ancient society with female strength at its core lived in the lands around the Black Sea nearly halfway between then and now. Female warriors who were masters of archery and horseback riding ruled sections of these lands. Early writers like Herodotus said they were tall and fierce in battle in the fifth century BCE, but Herodotus himself had never seen such women. His tales were games of Telephone in themselves. But myths often grow from reality, and the legend of the Amazons seems to be one more such truth.

In 2018, when remains of a female Scythian warrior, who died roughly 2,400 years ago, were uncovered in the Zaporozhye region of Ukraine, talk of Amazons and their reality spread across modern newspaper headlines like flickers of wildfire. In fact, graves of ancient warrior women have been discovered throughout Ukraine and Russia. Many of these burial mounds date back to the sixth through second century BCE, which lines up with both Homer's and later Herodotus's accounts about the nomadic tribes of the Scythians. These warrior women may also have been among the Sauromatians and early Sarmatians in nearby regions as well. The skeletal remains commonly discovered by present-day archeologists are female and have bowed legs, a sign of lives on horseback. Decorated bows and arrows, as well as swords, daggers, and bags of arrowheads are tucked within these women's graves, some of which also show signs of nobility with specialized ceramics and jewelry. Some of these skeletons are also a taller than average height as compared to women of this era. Ongoing archeological digs remind us that such female powerhouses were not matters of myth after all.

In *The Iliad*, Homer called these female warriors "equal to men," a rare epithet for a woman at this time in the Greek world, but one that has captured imaginations for millennia since. Lingering memories of these real-life heroines easily may have been the inspiration of personas like Maria Morevna, a character type that held fast within Eastern European storytelling with pride and a degree of mystique. Every lesson my mother ever taught me about the many ways a woman can be strong returns to mind as I think on these tales. Plus, remember, Baba Yaga too has the best of horses. She is nomadic with her moving home. She is usually peaceful, unless someone tries to take something of her own, in which case, she is the most fearsome of opponents.

We've seen how Baba Yaga transformed over millennia. The tales of the Amazons are no different. Not all regions of the world have stories of great women amid their foundation, but strong female figures of the past have their own ripple effects. And these warrior women were not the only ones.

During the reign of Peter the Great in Russia, a wooden decorative *lubok* (lubok being the singular of lubki) displayed the tsar in the form of an alligator being chased by a figure well understood to be Baba Yaga. Yes, political cartoons have a long, long history. The terrifying woman is wielding a pestle like a club and riding upon a boar. Most consider this Baba Yaga to be a parody of Peter's wife, Catherine, for this particular Baba Yaga is dressed in traditional Estonian clothing that matches Catherine's heritage. Why the alligator? Well, Peter had brought a stuffed alligator back from a European trip, and somehow the people latched onto the strange creature's connection to him. Tsar as alligator, Catherine as Baba Yaga. It doesn't sound like the happiest of marriages. But who would win the battle on the lubok? My money's on the formidable Baba Yaga, but that's me.

Nonetheless, his wife Catherine didn't begin the conversation about old witches in the tsar's family or Baba Yaga's presence during Peter the Great's reign—and if any confusion lingers around Catherine the Great, remember she was a different Catherine. Catherine the Great was Peter the Great's granddaughter. However, Peter's eldest half sister, Sofia Alekseyevna, made her own mark on the history of female aptitude and influence in the region.

Sofia may be a footnote in history books as the individual who acted as regent when Peter the Great officially became tsar as a young boy in 1682, but her story is much more complex than this detail. Not only was she regent of Russia for seven years, but she also did so in a time when, as a woman, she was not even permitted to attend the funeral of her father, Tsar Alexis, in 1676. Becoming a serious voice in politics would have been impossible to most. However, by leaving the *terem*, the separate living quarters for noblewomen in this time of Muscovite Russia, Sofia Alekseyevna stepped into the spotlight and international spheres of political influence. Much more could be said of her accusations and coups, but before her, the Russian society of her era would not have accepted a female ruler.

A number of great empresses, including Catherine the Great, soon followed her. In her own time, Sofia Alekseyevna became known as a strong-willed troublemaker, a woman unflinching and obsessed with power. Her detractors had a lot to say, as detractors do, but among their complaints include repeated references to Sofia as the witch Baba Yaga herself. Such intelligence, fearlessness, and determination in a woman must have been stained by something dark and unholy, they said. Hence, that's how her story would be popularly told, for we all know the power of a good story. People latch onto it, no matter what the truth may be. Sofia Alekseyevna was no angel, but she was no witch, just as the powerful Amazons were no figments of some ancient soldier's imagination.

Baba Yaga's legacy comes from goddesses. It comes from witch hunts. It comes from nomadic women of strength hidden within ancient Eastern European history. It comes from a lack of explanation, when a powerful woman steps into the scene unintimidated and ready to take action. Feminists have their many influences.

However, the young and the ambitious are far from the totality of Baba Yaga's story. The moon grows and becomes rounder. Similarly, the notorious woman in the woods has a mothering role as present as any other. In early derivations of Baba Yaga's tales, she has a long particular nose that can differentiate the freshest sacrifices to feed her daughters—and sometimes her granddaughters. In other traditions, she guides women through childbirth and nature through rebirth in the spring. When she is a giant ogress with a body that fills her entire hut, some tales whisper of a fetal position and the chicken-legged hut as nothing more or less than a womb. Anyone who found their way inside would begin their development, their true creation. Thus, to emerge was to be reborn.

Yvashka with the Bear's Ear did not harness his potential until spending time in Baba Yaga's hut. His friends were out hunting. He knew the old witch was coming. Yet inside that hut, all of the burgeoning pieces of who he could be took shape. When Baba Yaga finally arrived, he was a formidable foe.

The same can be said of Princess Katerina and Baba Yaga's daughter in their tale of the golden ring. If one survived her home, they were reborn into a new life on the other side.

Moreover, Baba Yaga's occasional role as mother extends far beyond her chicken-legged hut. A selflessness in her persists that may not be apparent at first glance. We see her boney legs and her iron teeth, forgetting that this old woman in the woods never ignores the children who come across her path. And after all, at her age, aren't we all children? Still, Baba Yaga feeds them; she gives them chores to further their development.

She challenges them to ensure arrogance and entitlement are never pieces of their personality. She gives them the freedom to discover themselves and their own abilities.

When a child is desperately in need, Baba Yaga plays the role of donor, fulfilling these desires—but only if they can prove themselves to be respectful, thoughtful, smart, brave, and kind. May all mothers have such steadfast love, dedication, and resolution.

Okay, fine. None of us would actually want Baba Yaga as a mother. However, her guiding principles are worth an extra moment of consideration—even if echoes of another historical Slavic woman from the 900s linger in her mothering style.

Princess Olga of Kiev often comes to my mind when considering Baba Yaga's brutal yet relentless depiction of maternity. As the first female ruler of the Kievan Rus', a federation of Slavic tribes, Olga acted as regent for her young son when her husband, Prince Igor, was killed by a neighboring tribe. She fiercely protected her people, so much so, as the story goes, she requested no money as tribute from her guilty neighbors, as was expected. She only asked for gifts of local pigeons and sparrows from the eves of every home. Once she received the birds and brought them home, she bound pieces of sulfur to their legs and released them, allowing the pigeons and sparrows to return home to their roosts within every building in the village where her husband was killed. Thus, every structure went up into flames, and the enemy tribe's home was destroyed. Is the story true? Oh, "The Russian Primary Chronicle," also called "The Chronicle of Nestor" or "The Kiev Chronicle," is full of legends and exaggerations, so I'm guessing not. Olga was later canonized after all, Saint Olga, patron saint of widows and converts, a protective mother and the grandmother to the man who raised Mokosh's statue then brought it down again in 988. As Baba Yaga knows, motherhood has no guidebook. The role is full of influence and complications.

Charles Perrault, collector and author of such fairytales as "Cinderella," "Sleeping Beauty," and "Puss in Boots," knew the power of motherhood too. He seized upon these strengths as he established the character Mother Goose, who became a renowned children's author herself—if *herself* is the proper pronoun for a fictional goose, sometimes woman, written by a late seventeenth-century man. Mother Goose can be playful in her nursery rhymes, but her words are unflinching in their own ways. Humpty Dumpty is shattered. The three blind mice lose their tails. In "Goosey, Goosey, Gander," an old man is thrown down the stairs. The origin and depth of Mother Goose are another book entirely, but when maternal figures and fowl's legs combine, I see a connection in the cultural zeitgeist.

Pigeons, sparrows, and geese aside, Baba Yaga also finds her balance between the woman she knows herself to be and the woman she needs to be for her children. Thus, her feminist ways empower, and her stamp on motherhood is twistedly inspirational, all while she meets the challenge of every parent: enabling one's young to become independent forces to be let loose in the world.

The old mother does not hover, nor does she fight her children's fights. She allows them to have their own failures and solve their own problems. She only steps in when absolutely necessary, such as when immortal wizards like Koscheii are a piece of the equation. A mother's got to do what a mother's got to do, after all.

Time as a parent can be like a race of Baba Yaga's three horsemen. They gallop past at breakneck speed: horseman in red for the dawn, horseman in white for the day, horseman in black for the night. Red, white, black. Red, white, black. I've heard tales in which Baba Yaga ages one year every time a child asks her a question, wrinkles rising, fragmenting the once smooth surface of her skin like tree roots exposed by eroding soil. Sure, her antediluvian appearance may be rectified by a tea of blue roses or a magic black sunflower, but the demands upon her take their toll. Baba Yaga understands these aspects of motherhood too.

Thus, as long as they respect her likewise, Baba Yaga treats each child the same, and time moves on. She ages from newly formed feminist to mother to crone. The full moon begins to wane. She and her house shift and bend but never break. Over her many years, she understands the value of having a house and a temperament that reposition as they have to, all while the world around her calls her a terror—she who is known to have human children but also offspring in the forms of bears and worms and wolves and maggots.

Wrinkles and scraggly white hairs indeed happen, but so does wisdom with all that time, and let us remember who likely first told so many of these tales. Would it not have been the grandmothers, the babas themselves, who helped raise the next generations? Mothers told their tales for sure, but mothers are—and always have been—torn between their myriad duties and responsibilities. Grandmothers, great aunts, and old neighbors had the time to sit and weave the stories for the children, as they sat with their mortars, pestles in hand, undertaking the time-consuming task of grinding flour from grain. From these female lips likely fell the first tales and their earliest evolutions. Thus, forest goddesses lingered in ogresses, and revered matriarchal societies hid within the astonishment of a chicken-legged house deep in the woods. By the time that printing presses established standard versions of these tales, the stories snagged and pulled in quite different directions, but the feminist, mother, and crone linger when we search for them. Fairytales capture the history of who we are and who we have been in the most magnificent of ways.

What is more, Perrault's entrance into this conversation is not merely connected with Mother Goose. One of his other famous narratives is the story of "Blue Beard," which might feel familiar amid our most recent Baba Yaga tale. In his popular fairytale, a young wife doesn't listen to her new husband's request to stay away from a dungeon door when he travels. The young woman, driven wild by curiosity, finally flings open the door, accidentally freeing a beast. We hear echoes across lands and time once again. Maria Morevna's tale is not an unfamiliar one, but the warrior queen's lead role is a twist all its own. As for which came first, we can only guess the history of oral traditions.

The first time I heard the story of Maria Morevna, I fell in love with the tale as if the women in my Slavic bloodline continued to whisper their knowledge of leadership, confidence, wisdom, strength, and steadfast resolution in the somehow already familiar words. My mother reminded me as often as she could how these aspects of female strength were and are a part of our Ukrainian heritage. When I grew and began to pay more attention, I realized Baba Yaga too was among these whisperers—for she is a feminist, a mother, and a crone, and in each of these capacities, she reminds her audiences of what women have been for millennia and what we may yet still be.

❧ 14 ❧

"BÁBA YAGÁ &
ZAMORÝSHEK"

he weight of something absent can drag down your very soul. Insides sunken with invisible but ever-present swallowed rocks, the old man knew such a feeling. He sank his ax into a long-ago chopped down tree, content to feel the solidity of at least something as his blade sliced into the wood that hadn't yet decayed.

Stretching his back, he let go of the handle. He could leave it for tomorrow, for who would steal an ax left in a forgotten tree? A passing stranger's whispered advice echoing in his ear, he strode away, a glimmer of hope allowing him to stand taller than he had in years.

Forty-one eggs he gathered together, one from every house in the village. He whispered the plan to his wife as their chicken roosted upon the tallest nest they'd ever seen, settling its feathers and its nerves. Settling the old man's and his wife's. By the next morning, the first cracks had begun, until forty-one shells had shattered and the old man and his wife had forty-one sons.

They put a hand to every head, giving each a powerful name, but by the time they reached the last, the smallest of them all, they had run out of ideas. They puzzled over this child, so different from the others, until they decided to call him Zamorýshek.

The forty-one boys grew by the minute and by the hour until they were young adults by afternoon. Their father called them to the field, forgetting his tiresome ax and picking up his pitchfork. His many sons used their many bare hands, and a month's work was done before supper.

"Wives," their mother called. "You need wives now that you're grown."

The boys nodded but turned at a clatter out in the fields to see Zamorýshek atop a sea green horse, a stampede of breathtaking steeds following behind him.

"One for each brother," Zamorýshek declared as he swung his leg off his mount. His horse's mane swayed like the far-off push and pull of the ocean's waves. He patted the creature's neck, and the handsome sea green horse nuzzled at his ear. "Wives?" he repeated, hearing his brothers' whispers. "We can leave to find them at dawn."

Thus, forty-one handsome brothers rode away on the most handsome forty-one horses the villagers had ever seen. They rode into lands their parents had never seen, across flat rocky steppes, across arid sandy foothills, and into forests as thick with foliage as haystacks with hay. In the midst of one such wood, amid the hornbeam, oak, and ash, a great gray stone castle emerged before them. The front door turned at their approach, or it could have been a trick of the eye, a trick of the shadows tugging against their tired attentions.

Forty-one pillars held iron loops to tie up forty-one horses, so the brothers decided the castle would be their perfect resting place for the night. When the last of the young men, Zamorýshek himself, touched his feet to the ground, Baba Yaga emerged from the heavy wooden door, framed with carvings of wolves and worms, maggots and bears.

"Are you here to do deeds," she called out, her voice scratchy with age or disuse, "or to run from them?"

"To do deeds!" the brothers answered as one.

"To find wives," Zamorýshek added.

"Why are you not inviting us inside for food and rest, old witch?" called out another, a brother Zamorýshek had recently started to despise.

Baba Yaga turned from Zamorýshek to the other who had spoken. Her elongated nose cast its own shadow. Her eyes were so dark they almost disappeared.

"Of course," she said. "Come in. Have a bath and rest yourselves. I will introduce you to my forty-one daughters, and we will feast."

The young men cheered, all but one, for Zamorýshek's horse, which he had pulled from the sea and once harnessed with a chain forged from the strongest blacksmith, nudged his ear. His brothers stampeded into the castle, bold and brash, their muddy boots flinging their journey's remains across the threshold. But the horse neighed and shook its sea green head, looking deep into Zamorýshek's eyes. And the young man suddenly knew. They would all die here.

But what was he to do but enter, wiping his feet, as his brothers had not done. He bathed and was introduced to the most beautiful daughter, her braids wrapped about the crown of her head as a diadem. When they dined, her movements were like a cat's, lithe and graceful, distrusting too, keeping her distance, ear tilted toward his words as if not daring to turn any more of herself toward him.

The brothers were all soon betrothed, but before they took to bed, Zamorýshek begged them each to end the night by going away with him, leaving their affianced behind dressed in the young men's clothes as a distraction and delay.

"You want to flee our wives?" said the one brother Zamorýshek despised.

"I want to flee with our lives," he answered as calmly as he could.

And in the end, his forty brothers begrudgingly listened, for they always knew Zamorýshek had more wiles and wisdom than them all. They whispered to their new beloveds where to find them, but none of them ever came—for in the same night, Baba Yaga ordered her servants to slay the forty-one brothers as they slept, handing them an ax to pass between them, beheading all who dared to disrespect her. Dressed in the brothers' clothes, Baba Yaga's daughters lost their lives one by one. And in the darkness, the servants placed their cloaked heads upon stakes to present to their mistress proudly the next morning.

Shortly after dawn, a wail swept through the forest like a gale, sweeping some brothers from their horses, forcing others to hang on for their lives as their steeds raced into sharp-leaved willow thickets around them.

At the lead was Zamorýshek, ready to part the sea so they could all escape the old witch he knew would soon be coming—for he understood what his father had once told him, how the weight of absence drags down your very soul, but he drew up short. At the edge of the forest was a familiar ax plunged into a tree. Its handle was worn with the grip of his own father. Zamorýshek guided his horse closer. Drips of sap were fresh from its placement. But not only sap, red smears tarnished the blade. Maple leaves rustled overhead, but Zamorýshek couldn't turn away. Closer now, he saw something familiar fastened at its end, a golden braid that had once designed itself as a diadem.

Another gust of wind howled. The sea wasn't near. Half his brothers had fallen.

Zamorýshek patted the ocean foam mane before him and tightened his grip on the reins. Great beings were born of eggs. Eagles. Dragons. The secret of Koscheii's immortality. Houses too, they say. Zamorýshek himself had emerged from a shell. If only he still had it for protection.

CHAPTER FOURTEEN

Horror & Escapism

Where the darkness stretches out its claws, there we find the essence of Baba Yaga. Or at least, that's the common understanding for those naïve to the old Slavic witch's world. To be fair, this assessment is absolutely true. She can be brutal and apathetic, ready to pinch a life away and use the leftover remnants of bones for her fence. She's stolen a bite out of the flesh of the disrespectful, and she's ripped young girls from the streets as they went about their day. Noir genres of books, television, and film allow us to explore the darkness within ourselves and the world around us. Then again, the pure horror of many Baba Yaga stories draws us to the final piece of our exploration.

Darkness exists, we know, but true horror is haunting, going beyond anxieties and into visceral revulsion and abhorrence. Jump scares and the absurdly unexpected allow for adrenaline rushes that many audiences find deeply satisfying. We all have our preferences. Not everyone is drawn to fictional media that raises neck hairs and such dramatic stakes. Moreover, psychological horror stories are different from those dripping with blood and gore. But escapism appears in many forms, and Baba Yaga habitually dips her bone-tipped toe into these chilly waters.

To be fair, the twist at the end of my telling of Zamorýshek's story was inspired from another tale, where a beheaded Baba Yaga, very much alive, escapes the scene by stretching out the long braids that had been woven over the crown of her head. The braids then transform into non-sensical legs that run her detached head away into the night. In a modern horror flick, this is likely the moment when audiences would argue the story went too far, but how can we ignore such a plot twist? Personally, I can't shake it from my mind, although I gave the braids less active participation. Cast across our sleeping eyes, the idea may very well jolt us awake at night, heart pounding, sweat upon our foreheads. Nightmares, we know, are never as simple as they seem. Yet again and again, people choose horror stories. *Frankenstein. Dracula. The Telltale Heart. The Haunting of Hill House. Psycho. The Exorcist. The Shining.* They are touchpoints in modern life as Baba Yaga also appears to be, even if the latter isn't always recognized as such.

Her existence has shifted and transformed over thousands of years in Eastern Europe, and the horror of that existence now crosses farther lands and seas, inspiring pen scratches and flurries of typed keys. Like anything that goes viral, the comprehensive backstory of the situation is hardly a necessity for the entertainment value. All the same, her absent-eyed stare and her relationship with the dead have come to life once again for new generations. Horror stories have their many appeals, and Baba Yaga checks each of these boxes, one by one.

To begin our list, we must face the truth that contemporary life can be predictable. Our alarm clocks are set. We have routines to our days—common breakfasts, regular commutes, standard errands, the same people crossing our paths amid their own cycles and grinds. But you know what I haven't seen? A house on chicken legs settling into its place and swinging open its door to release an old crone with a blacksmith-forged voice and bite. I've never seen a witch's tongue dangling from her perch in the air, snatching up anything that might satiate her hunger. These images are at once ridiculous and disconcerting, but isn't that a trademark of horror itself?

Our brains and bodily reactions are wired for threats. Flexing our survival instincts draws us closer to the core of who we as a human species have been before. Therefore, when Baba Yaga emerges, such ludicrous originality creates stimulation amid the monotony. The unexpected evokes an allure. Framed around modern media that separates true terror and our own safe spaces, boredom isn't a possibility.

Furthermore, Sigmund Freud suggested that people feel a catharsis after the buildup of extreme emotions and their sudden release, specifically, for example, through the experience of a false fear. The appeal of horror genres and extreme thrill-seeking alike relate to this idea. We are wound tighter and tighter. Stakes elevate our apprehensions. Situations become dire. Deadly. Ghastly. Then, as the resolution comes to be, our brains release endorphins that relax us, making us feel more comfortable in our surroundings and refreshed in a more profound capacity than we were before. The firebird saves Ivan the merchant's son from the youngest of the three baba yaga sisters who lunged, jaws spread. The captured boy once made of sticks squeezes out from the cage where he'd been confined, sprinkled with onions and dill. We triumph over dire circumstances, while safely distanced in our imaginations. A trick of the light, a trick of the brain.

This same concept leads to another draw of horror: facing dismay and distress together is known to forge deep bonds—no blacksmith needed. We know this is true for companions in war or amid unimaginable disasters. This reality simultaneously makes haunted houses and scary movies perfect for first dates. Similarly, Dmitri, the once-hedgehog boy, and Marusia will be a pair forevermore. Princess Katerina and Baba Yaga's daughter—the one that kept her head upon her shoulders—shall surely be inseparable for the rest of their lives. Prince Ivan, who sought the firebird for the tsar, will keep the hand of his Helena for together they faced Koscheii the Deathless and Baba Yaga herself.

Harnessing the ancient tradition of storytelling taps into communal bonding in the same way. Scary stories around a campfire or in the firelight of the hearth bring us closer through the act of listening together, not only for education or entertainment but also to live the shared experience.

The caveat is that we must remain vigilant concerning fearmongering for manipulation.

World leaders and media empires use horror tactics on a daily basis. This strategy is not at all a contemporary invention, but all around us, we feel it in play. Groups feel newly bonded, newly spurred into action, after listening to a captivating narrative meticulously crafted to deceive and to stir up emotions. The Spanish philosopher José Ortega y Gasset wrote *The Revolt of the Masses* in 1930, bringing awareness to such a situation, not in a context of horror but in the danger of a populace driven by emotion rather than thoughtful deliberation. That story does not end well, and the populist uprisings of today are not so different. The challenge of life and politics alike is and always has been knowing the difference when panic strikes our brains. The ability to press the pause button for attentive reflection is key.

In folktales, though, the horror is much simpler, albeit at times, more absurd. Thus, true horror enables a break from our ostensibly humdrum lives. It can evoke an emotional catharsis and establish greater bonds in our own relationships or between characters we empathize with as we consume their stories. The straightforward or subtle calls to action within are worth our attention. All the same, another hidden benefit of horror genres hides in a piece that Ortega's conclusions deem essential: someone listening to the story, reading the book, or watching the video can always create an intermission to take a breath. The break from the story is vital before jumping into action, but the pause also allows us to look around and recognize we are indeed okay in this moment.

Awareness that we can voluntarily enter and easily flee the scary environment furthers the escapist pleasure of frightening experiences. A first-date couple walking through a haunted house can stop and laugh, fingers touching, sparks flying to extreme levels because of the instinctual reactions firing in their brains. A flinch or gasp in a movie theater seat creates a psychological connectivity separate but not unrelated to that of comrades who have faced battle together. Alone in your house with the lights out, you can grab the remote and pause the Baba Yaga storyline. You can close your *Hellboy* comic or your book by Patricia McKillip or Gregory Maguire. Horror's appeals vary in intensity for audiences of different ages, after all. And this ability to walk away if you choose creates the illusion of mastery over anxiety-producing events. Who wouldn't want such command over any such stress or terror they meet in life? Is it a true command? Of course not, but your brain and its releasing endorphins don't care about that. Self-attained safety feels good.

Still, we know safety isn't forever. We know tranquility comes and goes. We build up walls around that which scares us, even restricting thoughts of our human fragility to hospices and hospitals. Medical advances have almost allowed us to forget about the everyday nature of death and dying. We forget about our own mortality. Respect for a once-goddess who guided souls into this world or out of it is such a strange idea to us, because such a being would never walk the halls of sterilized, fluorescent-lit medical buildings.

Stories have always sought to explain that which we cannot comprehend—especially that which terrifies us. Nevertheless, our collective memory doesn't always hold on to the original intentions. We don't sing, "ring around the rosy, pocket full of posies," thinking about the smell of flowers to cover up the smell of the dead. We consider it a playful nonsense rhyme. We ignore the horrors of babies rocking in cradles on treetops with boughs breaking and thus cradles falling. We don't overthink the man who sleeps, snoring, while it's raining and pouring, even after he hits his head and doesn't wake up again.

The horrible exists. In different eras of human life and in different societies around the world, we have confronted these horrors in different ways. None are necessarily right or wrong, but comparing our reactions and responses today to other times gives us more to consider. Ortega might appreciate all of these extra moments of thoughtful consideration.

Baba Yaga's multidimensional presence weaves in and out of folk-tales, but her worst self thrives in contemporary stories—in the dark alleyways of a busy city, in the wood where her effigy is carved into a rock, in a broken-down house at the edge of town, or wherever we might find her. She calls us back to the morbidity of human existence, the ugliness of the world, and the terror that hides in powerful emotions.

Life can be anxiety-inducing and petrifying sometimes. Perhaps the final appeal of horror genres and Baba Yaga tales is their role as exposure therapy. They force stress levels to heighten and situations to seem dire to enable us to comprehend our own capacity for survival. Puzzling out solutions, escapes, traps, and paths to freedom can feel like practice runs for tumultuous times to come, although our real tumultuous times hopefully don't involve iron-jawed witches or servants who behead in the night.

We see Baba Yaga herself face horror after horror as well, not all of which are her own creation. Her eyes are tarred shut. She is attacked by all the birds of the world. She falls into a river of fire to burn, but like fields razed to stimulate future growth or rich volcanic soil born of eruption, she is not at the end of her story. Baba Yaga knows that she and only she can answer any challenge, and in witnessing her confidence in the face of deathless wizards or clever young heroines alike, we too emerge capable of facing anything.

Where the darkness stretches out its claws, there we find the essence of Baba Yaga. She's so much more than this, but this alone creates so much of her fascination. Will she catch Zamorýshek at the end of his story? Will she catch you at the end of yours? Who's to say? Heart beating fast, endorphins on the rise, remember the pause button is always there if and when you need it.

15

"THE BRAVE YOUTH"

hen the sparrow and the cat left the brave youth alone in their small house, they always reminded the child to be good.

"Do not poke twigs into the fire," the sparrow said. "Do not whittle with the knives or throw rocks at the crooked crabapple tree where the fire ants live."

"And if Baba Yaga comes to count our spoons," the cat added, flicking its tail, "be tranquil and silent."

With that, the sparrow flew out the open window, and the cat leapt after him, stretching her legs to dash across the tangled foxtail and wool-fruited sedge. More wood from the forest was needed for their fire.

The brave youth traced a finger through wood shavings left behind from the work of the cat's sharp claws. The child tidied the seed recently spilled by the sparrow. But only a moment more passed before the small house's front door creaked open. Cast in shadow by the slanted light of the morning sun stood Baba Yaga, the boney legged. The old witch didn't acknowledge the brave youth. She lifted her long nose and hobbled to the kitchen table. The brave youth had tidied the seed, but three spoons remained out, freshly cleaned after the morning's meal.

"A spoon for the sparrow," Baba Yaga whispered, touching her long, boney finger to the first spoon. "A spoon for the cat," she continued, tapping her finger on the second spoon. "And a spoon for—"

The brave youth bit their lip, trying not to speak. But tranquil and silent wasn't something easy to be.

"Don't touch my spoon!"

Baba Yaga met the brave youth's eyes, and in the same instant, the old witch swept the child up, depositing them both in her giant mortar, and together, they flew away.

The brave youth hollered for help. The child wailed. The child screamed.

Hearing the calls, the sparrow and cat rushed to help, beak and claws sharpened. They launched themselves at the old witch who flew low over the forest's trees, magical broom following behind, sweeping away any trail. But screams couldn't be swept away as easily.

After seeing the cat and sparrow, the brave youth crouched lower against the smooth stone bowl of the massive mortar, eyes squeezed shut until the moment of tumbling free.

The brave youth should have learned. The cat had hissed and spit. The sparrow had thrashed his wings. But again, when Baba Yaga came to their home while the guardians were away, the brave youth was not silent.

Baba Yaga whisked the child away again, too far and too fast this time for the cat and sparrow to hear any scream. Their fast-moving shadow chased them on the treetops far below, over aspens, ancient beech, and stone pines.

The bump of their landing bounced the brave youth from the mortar to land in a patch of soft, spring-green moss. The witch's daughter sat by a slanted old hut nearby. She clearly waited for Baba Yaga's return, standing immediately as the old witch turned her way.

"Cook my dinner," Baba Yaga shrieked to the scraggly haired girl, prodding the brave youth with her bare boney toe.

The daughter nodded as her mother took again to her mortar, pestle in hand, and flew away. She stepped forward to examine the brave youth that would become the evening's meal then pulled out a large pan and ordered her guest to lie down within it.

Trembling, the brave youth climbed upon the metal pan but stuck one leg straight up toward the sky.

"Like this?"

"No, no, no," the daughter scowled. "Not like that."

The brave youth squatted on the pan, arms splayed out like wings, pulling inspiration from the chicken-legged hut that had stretched to stand beside them as if to get a better look.

"No!" the daughter shrieked, not unlike her mother.

"How then?" the brave youth questioned, keeping as straight a face as possible.

Rolling her eyes, the daughter pushed her guest out of the pan, climbing in herself to show how to fit properly. She lay down upon her back, folding her hands together upon her stomach. The brave youth threw open the oven door and pushed the pan inside.

For a cat can be fierce and a bird can take flight, but voices aren't meant to be silenced. Spoons are merely spoons until the day they are more. Bravery comes in all shapes, though none pan-sized.

CHAPTER FIFTEEN

The Contemporary Lure
of Baba Yaga

Certain stories linger in the modern psyche, stories that have been around for a long, long time. Epics about historic floods exist not only in the Bible, but also in the tales of Gilgamesh and the Sumerian "Eridu Genesis" among many others, making historians, literary scholars, and archeologists alike curious about the specific world events that may have sparked these narratives. Theories arise about the heavy occurrence of dinosaur bones on the Asian steppes as one possible source of hybrid animal mythologies—with the structure of triceratops skeletons, a common finding in this region, looking a great deal like mythical griffins, body of a lion and head of an eagle. Other dinosaur bones could have inspired tales of dragons long before ideas of mass extinctions took hold.

Stories grow. Stories linger. What has Baba Yaga shown us but this?

Like the sieve she often gives a young protagonist as a test, demanding girls like Natasha to fill a tub while well-water leaks away with every passing step, this ancient Slavic witch's record itself has countless holes. Only drops of how Baba Yaga has become Baba Yaga remain in every retelling. The bathtub is impossible to fill. Or is it?

Today, you might hear stubborn arguments about the pronunciation of her name. Emphasizing the first or second syllable of "Yaga" is at the top of this list. "Baba YaGA" or "Baba YAga." Oh, did I make you say it aloud? My Ukrainian heritage argues for emphasis on the first syllable, but regional differences are real. Baba Yaga stretches her long-armed reach across much of Eastern Europe, across multiple languages and accents.

As with all language considerations, let's not argue. Let's dig through the roots and dust instead. That's always been my philosophy, for the digging unearths the intrigue. "Curse words," for example, have their origins in the Old English word *cursian*, as far back as the 12th century, meaning "to wish evil upon" or "an incantation of ill will." Yes, sorcery and dark magic hide within profanities. I've also always appreciated the idea that well-chosen words can cast spells upon their audience. That, after all, is why we call it "spelling." Thanks, Bruce Lee, for that one.

The power of language and stories has fascinated me for as long as I can remember. Perhaps because English was not my mother's first language, we spoke of language quirks and subtleties frequently, and I have been blessed with numerous storytellers in my life, those who tended toward the dark realities of lived-through wars and those who dabbled with more creativity. My father whispered bedtime stories about warrior princesses for years, although admittedly, I didn't learn of Maria Morevna until much later on. My love of her story could easily be connected to these earliest of memories.

However, I am not the same as I was at six years old or at sixteen. Nor are you. We could all be stronger if we considered all the people we have been and how they all have shaped us into who we have become. Baba Yaga is no different. Her history is not hundreds but thousands of years old. How can we expect an old hag in a *Scooby Doo* episode to capture her complexities? No singular episode defines you. We should give her legacy the same courtesy.

The simplistic and the frivolous combine when the brave youth is so opinionated about those spoons, but why shouldn't we fight for that which nurtures us? Every tale has something to say between the ink and the absence. The brave youth reminds us of the necessity of raising our voices when needed—and our limbs too, I suppose. Staying calm and thinking quickly do tend to lead us toward our best results, whether Baba Yaga is present or not.

Whatever intention brought you to this book, I'll again pose the same question that Baba Yaga favors: have you come to do deeds or run from them?

Becoming the protagonist of your own life is not a matter for a narrator to decide. Your setting and backstory don't determine your fate. You can do deeds, or you can run from them. You can have your free will, showing up of your own accord, or arrive compelled by others. Baba Yaga is far wiser than her reputation acknowledges.

The old Slavic witch's history settles over her stories like an enchantment. With determination, bravery, cleverness, and kind hearts, we too might be able to seek out her truths, as so many characters have through the ages. Maybe we can, even if we don't have contemporary animals of the forest to help. Still, I might be in the market for a pet hedgehog—survivor of venom, killer of snakes, creature as in tune with the darkness and forest as Baba Yaga herself.

If someone holding a skull aloft brings to mind Hamlet, forevermore, please consider the same image with a candle inside, held by young Vasilisa as she makes her way home through the forest.

And may you never look at the erratic movements of scrawny-legged chickens in the same light.

The fantastical imagination of it all could have come from the mouth of a storyteller so long ago, we don't remember her name, and all the storytellers of the centuries since have added their own twists to the tale— one more bone built along the fence, protecting the old crone and her solitude.

We all want our privacy, though bone fences aren't required. We search for ways to shift the narrative, and all the while, Baba Yaga whispers through the centuries that we can always tear it all down and start over again. The plow tumbles the solid earth. The witch of the forest rips open the fields, diving down deep to find the forgotten lands hidden underneath.

True, the savagery of a Baba Yaga philosophy is not quite the approach we truly need, but as she attempts to scare the world into becoming a better place, we can't say that we don't see where she is coming from. She is a brutal teacher, inflexible and demanding, but through her challenges, characters discover stronger versions of themselves. Readers and listeners do too. Self-help books come in many forms, after all.

Our modern era demands simple explanation after the sound bite—quick analysis after a few minutes of research. We read the headlines but not the story. Thus, Baba Yaga is commonly no more and no less than a terrifying Slavic witch, a "boogeyman," to borrow a highly disputed translation from the John Wick franchise.

Yet through it all, Baba Yaga is not only a character colliding with modernity. She has been relevant to contemporary life throughout her entire existence. Her appearance in movies, television, video games, and popular spiritual culture today is no rise from the ashes. Baba Yaga has lurked on the fringes of consciousness for centuries, waiting in her hut deep in the woods for the next hero or heroine to stumble upon her, reminding us always:

Head down, child, as you cut your way through the forest. Don't disturb the creatures there or the plants emerging from the soil.

Walk fast, young man, when you stray where you should not go, then return to the path warmed by the light of the sun.

Stop bickering with each other, children and adults, or Baba Yaga will get you.

Don't agree to those "Terms and Conditions" without reading them for you might be promising away your soul.

Okay, I might have made that last one up. But you have to know what monsters are after you if you want to avoid them. The monsters might hide in the fine print and the deep fake you didn't spot, but who other than Baba Yaga could really say?

A retelling of a story is more than a matter of stealing it. For folktales, these retellings speak to the legacies of those who came before us, all they believed, and the hopes and dreams they left us to ponder. Legacies can be complicated, and Baba Yaga's is an amalgamation of ancient stories and imagination, all coaxed into who we know her as today.

She is a character that has slipped from Slavic culture into worldwide fascination and fandom. No "correct" version of Baba Yaga exists, because she has been countless identities over time, always reminding us that the world is a place of concurrent hope and fear. Finding a way to navigate through the sunshine and the shadows is the hero's journey set out before us. And all the while, Baba Yaga is out there, embracing the possibilities—hers, of course, but our own as well.

Author's Note

The evolution of a story mirrors the evolution of language itself. Both are the product of the people who speak them. Trends arise. History shapes them. But as social constructions, they are persistently, stubbornly fluid. They can be deeply analyzed and hypothesized, but no one can wend their way to a singular answer for every subtlety. Conjecture itself has its own faults and biases.

Much of the research around Eastern European folktales has a pro-Soviet or pro-Russian slant going back hundreds of years, while other academics and casual observers alike lean into the romanticism of nature or that of a mystical female spiritualism. I tried in my own efforts to explore widely and remain diligent and thoughtful in my own widespread and meticulous examinations. Baba Yaga tales were not separated by rural versus urban backdrops, nor were they separated by social hierarchy, national borders, or language itself. No singular version exists of who she is or who she was. All forms of her simultaneously clash and merge as one.

I have known Baba Yaga since I was a child. I have studied her in Russian literature courses and countless international translations. Diving into this character and how her presence has become so widespread over time has been an experience at once fulfilling and fascinating for me. My Ukrainian roots have danced to the surface of my daily life through my extensive research, but I'm fully aware that my personal heritage owns but one piece of her story.

The evolution of language has no linear path. Storytelling is the same. The history of storytelling is a narrative, and we are but heroes on this journey. If you make a choice that would bring the old witch's ire, that could be your end. Another brave youth lost in the darkness. A quest incomplete. A story that lingers as a reminder to others. Or maybe, your epic will take another turn entirely.

Baba Yaga brings us the horrific and anxiety-inducing in a visceral way while reminding us that those who are disciplined, who strive to do their best, who are brave, and who are smart are the ones the old Slavic witch allows to continue on their journey. Let us all be so, and she may even give us a skull of fire to light our way. What happens next is up to you.

Selected Bibliography

Afanas'ev, Alexandr. *Russian Fairy Tales*. Translated by Norbert Guterman, commentary by Roman Jakobson. New York: Pantheon Books, 1945.

Armknecht, Megan, Jill Terry Rudy, and Sibelan Forrester. "Identifying Impressions of Baba Yaga: Navigating the Uses of Attachment and Wonder on Soviet and American Television." *Marvels & Tales* 31, no. 1 (2017): 62–79. Wayne State University Press.

Birkenmayer, Sigmund S. "N. A. Nekrasov: a glimpse of the man and the poet." *Études Slaves et Est-Européennes / Slavic and East-European Studies*, Vol. 12, No. 4 (Hiver/Winter 1967/68): 188–200. Canadian Association of Slavists.

Ciepielak, Ivonka. "Divine Siblings? The Pre-Christian Ancestry of Baba Yaga and the Black Madonna of Czestochowa." University of Amsterdam, 2018.

Dugan, Frank. "Baba Yaga and the Mushrooms." *FUNGI Magazine*, 10 (2017): 6–18.

———. "Fungi, Folkways and Fairy Tales: Mushrooms & Mildews in Stories, Remedies & Rituals, from Oberon to the Internet." *North American Fungi*, 3 (2008): 23–72.

Gimbutas, Marija Alseikaitė. *The Civilization of the Goddess: the World of Old Europe*. San Francisco: HarperSanFrancisco, 1991.

———. "The Earth Fertility Goddess of Old Europe." *Dialogues d'Histoire Ancienne*, (1987): 11–69.

Guseva, Irina S., Vladimir G. Ivanov, and Maria G. Ivanova. "In Search of the Archetype: From the Mother Archetype to the Archetype of Baba Yaga." *Studia Mythologica Slavica* 22 (2019).

Illes, Judika. *Encyclopedia of Spirits: The Ultimate Guide to the Magic of Saints, Angels, Fairies, Demons, and Ghosts (Witchcraft & Spells).* San Francisco: HarperOne, 2009.

Ivanits, Linda J. *Russian Folk Belief.* Armonk, NY: M. E. Sharpe, Inc., 1989.

Johns, Andreas. "Baba Iaga and the Russian Mother." *The Slavic and East European Journal,* Vol. 42, No. 1 (Spring, 1998): 21–36.

———. *Baba Yaga: The Ambiguous Mother and Witch of the Russian Folktale.* Peter New York: Lang Publishing, Inc., 2010.

"Katharine Pyle Papers, Helen Farr Sloan Library & Archives, Delaware Art Museum," Purchased from Oak Knoll Books, 1996.

Kovtun, Valeria. "Trypillia: 7000-year-old civilisation [sic] silenced by communists." BBC Reel (film), 10 June 2021.

Lobachev, Sergey. "Indexes in Cyrillic imprints in early modern Ukraine and Russia." *The Indexer: The International Journal of Indexing* 1 (2020): 11–28.

Machemer, Theresa. "Tomb Containing Three Generations of Warrior Women Unearthed in Russia." *Smithsonian Magazine,* December 30, 2019.

Murashko, Olga, Nikolai Krenke, and Mila Bonnichsen. "Burials of Indigenous People in the Lower Ob Region: Dating, Burial Ceremonies, and Ethnic Interpretations." *Arctic Anthropology,* Vol. 33, No. 1 (1996): 37–66. University of Wisconsin Press.

Nekrasov, Nikolay Alexandrovich. "Baba Yaga the bony leg." *Dreams and Sounds,* 1840.

Nestor. *The Russian Primary Chronicle: Laurentian Text.* Edited and translated by Samuel Hazzard Cross and Olgerd P. Sherbowitz-Wetzor. Cambridge, MA, 1953.

Pallua, Jelka Vince. "A Newly Discovered Figurative Representation of the Mythical Baba – 'Old Baba Vukoša' in St. Mary's Church of Gračišće in Istria." *Sacralization of Landscape and Sacred*

Places (June 2016): 104–116. Institute of Archaeology, Zagreb, Croatia.

Propp, Vladimir Yakovlevich. "Historical Roots of a Magical Fairy Tale." Translated by Christopher Michael Coffey. Western Washington University, 1997.

Ransome, Arthur. *Old Peter's Russian Tales*. London: Thomas Nelson and Sons Ltd., 1916.

Rjabchikov, Sergei V. "The Scytho-Sarmatian Mythology and the Slavonic Folklore." Sergei Rjabchikov Foundation, Research Centre for Studies of Ancient Civilisations and Cultures in Krasnodar, February 9, 2021.

Roatcap, Adela. "Lubki: The Wood Engravings of Old Russia." *Parenthesis, Journal of the Fine Press Book Association*, No. 10 (November 2004).

The Russian Fairy Book. Translated by Nathan Haskell Dole, Illustrated by Ivan Yakovlevich Bilibin. New York: Crowell, 1907.

Russian Wonder Tales. Translated by George Post Wheeler, Illustrated by Ivan Yakovlevich Bilibin. New York: The Century Co., 1912.

Small, E., Lent, B. & B. *Baba Yaga*. Boston: Houghton Mifflin, 1966.

Stratulat, Lăcrămioara, ed. "Cucuteni – Trypillia: A Great Civilization of Old Europe," Exhibition Catalogue, Palazzo della Cancelleria, Rome-Vatican, 16 September – 31 October 2008. Ministry of Culture and Religious Affairs of Romania, Ministry of Culture and Tourism of Ukraine, with Special Contribution of the Republic of Moldova.

Strickland, Ashley. "Three generations of ancient Amazon women warriors found in Russian tomb." *CNN.com*, January 6, 2020.

Valentsova, M. "Is the Russian Baba-Yaga related to the Greek Echidna?" *Kathedra of Byzantine and Modern Greek Studies*, Society of Modern Greek Studies (Russia) No. 14-1 (2023): 57–66.

Videiko, Mykhailo. "The 'disappearance' of Trypillia culture." *Documenta Praehistorica XXXVIII* (2011). Institute of Archaeology, National Academy of Sciences, Kyiv, Ukraine.

———. "Trypillia Civilization in Prehistory of Europe." Kyiv Domain Archaeological Museum, Institute of Archaeology, National Academy of Sciences of Ukraine, Kyiv, 2005.

Wilford, John Noble. "Ancient Graves of Armed Women Hint at Amazons." *New York Times.* February 25, 1997, Section C page 1.

Wise, Thomas, ed. "The Story of Yvashka with the Bear's Ear." Translated by George Borrow (original pamphlet printed for private circulation). 1913. The Project Gutenberg eBook.

Zamyatin, Evgeny. "Letter to Stalin." *A Soviet Heretic: Essays.* Chicago & London: The University of Chicago Press, 1970.

ABOUT THE AUTHOR

Kris Spisak understands that well-written words and well-told stories can change the world. She wrote her first three books—*Get a Grip on Your Grammar: 250 Writing and Editing Reminders for the Curious or Confused* (Career Press, 2017), *The Novel Editing Workbook* (Davro Press, 2020), and *The Family Story Workbook* (Davro Press, 2020)—to help writers of all kinds sharpen their storytelling and empower their communications. Her "Grammartopia" and "Story Stop Tour" events follow the same mission.

Her first novel, *The Baba Yaga Mask* (Wyatt-MacKenzie Publishing, 2022; Tantor Audio, 2023)—called "a complex, poetic tale" by Kirkus Reviews—is a dual timeline quest through Eastern Europe inspired by the post-WWII Ukrainian diaspora stories Kris has heard from family and friends her entire life as well as Slavic folktales and the artistic traditions of Ukrainian culture. Her fifth book, *Becoming Baba Yaga* (Hampton Roads Publishing, 2024) returns to nonfiction, combining Kris's love of storytelling, Slavic culture, and deep historical and linguistic research, with a twist of self-empowerment and the macabre.

Kris is a graduate of the College of William and Mary (BA) and the University of Richmond (MLA). She has been spotlighted in *Writer's Digest* and *The Huffington Post* for her work dedicated to helping other writers and storytellers, and she is passionate about transforming book signings and storytelling events into humanitarian aid efforts when the opportunity allows. When she is not working on her own projects or immersed in an intriguing tale, she is an active speaker, workshop leader, and creative strategist. Otherwise, she's likely taking walks in the woods, especially in the Appalachian Mountains of her childhood, and traveling as much as she can.

TO OUR READERS